CHOCOLATE
heaven

CHOCOLATE *heaven*

75 IRRESISTIBLE CREATIONS

CHRISTINE FRANCE

This edition is published by Lorenz Books, an imprint of Anness Publishing Ltd,
Blaby Road, Wigston, Leicestershire LE18 4SE; info@anness.com

www.lorenzbooks.com; www.annesspublishing.com

If you like the images in this book and would like to investigate using them for publishing, promotions or advertising, please visit our website www.practicalpictures.com for more information.

Publisher: Joanna Lorenz
Senior Cookery Editor: Linda Fraser
Cookery Editor: Rosemary Wilkinson
Designer: Annie Moss
Mac Artist: John Fowler
Photography: Steve Baxter
Food for Photography: Jane Stevenson
Styling: Diana Civil

© Anness Publishing Ltd 2013

PUBLISHER'S NOTE
Although the advice and information in this book are believed to be accurate and true at the time of going to press, neither the authors nor the publisher can accept any legal responsibility or liability for any errors or omissions that may have been made nor for any inaccuracies nor for any loss, harm or injury that comes about from following instructions or advice in this book.

NOTES
Bracketed terms are intended for American readers.
For all recipes, quantities are given in both metric and imperial measures and, where appropriate, in standard cups and spoons. Follow one set of measures, but not a mixture, because they are not interchangeable.
Standard spoon and cup measures are level. 1 tsp = 5ml, 1 tbsp = 15ml, 1 cup = 250ml/8fl oz.
Australian standard tablespoons are 20ml. Australian readers should use 3 tsp in place of 1 tbsp for measuring small quantities.
American pints are 16fl oz/2 cups. American readers should use 20fl oz/2.5 cups in place of 1 pint when measuring liquids.
Electric oven temperatures in this book are for conventional ovens. When using a fan oven, the temperature will probably need to be reduced by about 10–20°C/20–40°F. Since ovens vary, you should check with your manufacturer's instruction book for guidance.
Medium (US large) eggs are used unless otherwise stated.

CONTENTS

$\mathcal{I}$NTRODUCTION

Few foods are as rich, sensuous and wickedly
tempting as chocolate. Whether you nibble it,
savour it or simply surrender to its charms,
chocolate is pure pleasure. There's something
almost addictive about this gift of the gods, as
anyone who has ever tried to give it up,
however briefly, will testify.

*T*he ultimate decadent treat, it is hardly surprising that in the past chocolate has been credited with being an aphrodisiac. Chocolates are traditional lovers' gifts, and special events, such as Easter and Christmas, are celebrated with chocolate eggs or the traditional yuletide log.

Once the preserve of Aztec emperors, highly prized and coveted, chocolate was unknown in Europe until the middle of the 16th century, when it was introduced as a rare and wonderful beverage. It took almost two hundred years before the sweetened chocolate bar made its appearance, and the rest, as they say, is history. Although chocolate is now accessible to all, familiarity has done nothing to dim its popularity. Consumption of all types of chocolate continues to rise. In recent years there has been an increased demand for the pure product with more than 50 per cent cocoa solids, and foodies scout out new varieties of chocolate with all the enthusiasm and energy of the ardent wine buff or truffle fancier.

For the cook, the fascination with chocolate goes even deeper. It is a sensitive ingredient which needs careful handling, but which offers remarkable rewards. The velvety texture and rich flavour add a touch of luxury to numerous cakes, cookies, puddings and desserts, and it is equally good in hot or cold dishes. As an added bonus, chocolate can be piped, shaped and moulded to make a variety of exciting decorations. Full instructions, with detailed advice on a range of other techniques, are included in the introduction.

This is a book for serious chocolate lovers. As you would expect, we've included classics like Black Forest Gâteau and Double Chocolate Chip Muffins, but – and this is the mark of the true chocoholic – we've also investigated every conceivable way of introducing our favourite ingredient into familiar and much-loved dishes. There's a rich chocolate trifle, a rare chocolate pavlova (with

cocoa giving the meringue a dusky appearance and delectable flavour), an unusual chocolate crème brulée, a chocolate zabaglione and even a chocolate and cherry polenta cake.

Basic advice includes instructions for making chocolate pastry, and for those who really don't believe you can get too much of a good thing, there are double delights like Tiramisu in Chocolate Cups, White Chocolate Vanilla Mousse with Dark Chocolate Sauce and Steamed Chocolate and Fruit Puddings with Chocolate Syrup.

Also in the luscious line-up are easy to make recipes like crunchy chocolate chip cookies and chocolate sponge cakes with fudgy centres. There are also gloriously gooey puddings, voluptuous gâteaux and sweet chocolate treats for gifts and after-dinner delights. In honour of those ancient Aztecs, there's a recipe for Mexican Hot Chocolate and even an iced chocolate and peppermint drink.

TYPES OF CHOCOLATE

COUVERTURE
The professionals' choice, this is a fine quality pure chocolate with a high percentage of cocoa butter, which gives it a high gloss. It is suitable for decorative use and for making handmade chocolates. Couverture is expensive and must generally be tempered before use (see page 13). Specialist shops sell couverture chocolate.

PLAIN DARK CHOCOLATE
Often called "luxury", "bitter" (semisweet) or "Continental" (European) chocolate, this has a high percentage of cocoa solids – around 75 percent – with little or no added sugar. Many people find plain dark chocolate too bitter for eating, but its rich, intense flavour and good dark colour make it an ideal ingredient in desserts or cakes.

PLAIN (UNSWEETENED) CHOCOLATE
Plain chocolate is the most widely available chocolate to use in cooking. It contains anywhere between 30 and 70 percent cocoa solids, so check the label before you buy. The higher the cocoa solids, the better the flavour.

MILK CHOCOLATE
This contains powdered or condensed milk and sugar, and generally has only 20 percent cocoa solids. Although this is the most popular eating chocolate, it is not as suitable as plain chocolate for melting and cooking.

WHITE CHOCOLATE
This does not contain any cocoa solids, but gets its flavour from cocoa butter. It is sweet, and the better quality white chocolate is quite rich and smooth. White chocolate must be melted with care as it does not withstand heat as well as plain chocolate and is liable to stiffen if allowed to get too hot.

CHOCOLATE CHIPS
These are small pieces of chocolate of uniform size, convenient for stirring directly into biscuit dough or cake mixture, or for melting. Chocolate chips contain fewer cocoa solids than ordinary chocolate, and are available in plain dark, plain, milk and white.

COCOA
This is made from the pure cocoa mass after most of the cocoa butter has been extracted and has no added sugar. The mass is roasted, then ground to make a powder. It is probably the most economical way of giving puddings and baked goods a chocolate flavour.

ORGANIC CHOCOLATE
This is slightly more expensive than other types of chocolate but is a quality product, high in cocoa solids, produced without pesticides and with consideration for the environment. Dark, milk and flavoured varieties are available.

CHOCOLATE-FLAVOUR CAKE COVERING
This is a blend of sugar, vegetable oil, cocoa and flavourings. As its name suggests, it should only be used for covering or decoration as the flavour is poor. However, the high fat content makes it suitable for making chocolate curls or caraque – to improve the flavour, melt a few squares with good plain chocolate.

TECHNIQUES

Melting Chocolate

There are basically three ways to melt chocolate:

USING A DOUBLE BOILER

1 Fill the base of a double boiler or saucepan about a quarter full. Fit the top pan or place a heatproof bowl over the saucepan. The water should not touch the top container. Bring the water to just below boiling point, then turn down the heat to the lowest possible setting.

2 Break the chocolate into squares and place in the top pan or bowl. Leave to melt completely, without stirring. Keep the water at a very slow simmer.

TIPS FOR MELTING CHOCOLATE

- Melt chocolate slowly, as overheating will spoil both the flavour and texture.
- Avoid overheating – dark chocolate should not be heated above 49°C/120°F; milk and white chocolate should not go above 43°C/110°F.
- Never allow water or steam to come into contact with melting chocolate, as this may cause it to stiffen.
- Do not cover chocolate after melting, as condensation could cause it to stiffen.

MELTING IN THE MICROWAVE

Break the chocolate into squares and place it in a bowl suitable for use in the microwave. Heat until just softened – chocolate burns easily in the microwave, so check often, remembering that chocolate retains its shape when melted in this way.

Approximate times for melting plain (unsweetened) or milk chocolate in a 650-700 watt microwave oven:

115g/4oz	2 minutes on High (100% power)
200-225g/7-8oz	3 minutes on High (100% power)
115g/4oz white chocolate	2 minutes on Medium (50% power)

DIRECT HEAT METHOD

This is only suitable for recipes where the chocolate is melted in other liquids, such as milk or cream. Break up the chocolate into a saucepan. Add the liquid, then heat gently, stirring occasionally, until the chocolate has melted and the mixture is smooth.

Storing Chocolate

Chocolate keeps well if stored in a cool, dry place, away from strong smelling foods. Check "best before" dates on the pack.

Tempering Chocolate

Couverture (pure chocolate with no fats other than cocoa butter) must be tempered to distribute the cocoa fat evenly and produce a glossy finish. It is useful for decorations or for moulding.

1 Break up the chocolate
~ into pieces and place it
in the top of a double boiler
or a heatproof bowl over a
saucepan of hot water. Heat
gently until just melted.

2 Tip about three-quarters
~ of the chocolate on to a
marble slab or a cool,
smooth work surface.

3 With a flexible plastic
~ scraper or palette knife,
spread the chocolate thinly,
then scoop it up, keeping it
constantly on the move, for
about 5 minutes.

4 Using a chocolate
~ thermometer, check the
temperature of the chcolate
as you work it. As soon as it
registers 28°C/82°F, tip the
chocolate back into the
bowl and stir into the
remaining chocolate.

5 With the addition of
~ the hot chocolate, the
temperature should now
be 32°C/90°F, and the
chocolate is ready to use. To
test, drop a little chocolate
on to the marble; it should
set very quickly.

Chocolate Decorations

All these decorations can be made using plain, milk or white chocolate.

GRATED CHOCOLATE

Using a coarse cheese grater
or the grating blade of a

food processor, grate a large
bar of chocolate. Grated
chocolate is useful for
sprinkling over desserts or
cakes, or coating the sides of
gâteaux. If you use a cheese
grater, stand it on a sheet of
non-stick baking paper for
extra convenience. The
grated chocolate can then
be easily tipped or brushed
off as required.

QUICK CHOCOLATE CURLS

Use a swivel bladed
vegetable peeler to shave
curls of chocolate from the
whole bar. This works best
when the chocolate has
been brought to room
temperature.

*E*QUIPMENT

Working with chocolate requires little by way of special equipment. Most items will be found in any well-stocked kitchen, but you may need to buy one or two extra pieces of equipment if you plan to mould chocolates.

CHEESE SLICER
The blade is drawn across a thin layer of just set chocolate to make curls or caraque.

CHOCOLATE MOULDS
Most small chocolate moulds are made from flexible plastic, though some larger ones, such as Easter egg moulds, are made from polished metal.

CHOCOLATE OR CANDY THERMOMETER
Mainly used for tempering chocolate, this is a specialist item.

CHOCOLATE TOOLS
Professionals use these for dipping and marking chocolates. Buy them from specialist cake decorating suppliers.

COCKTAIL STICKS (TOOTHPICKS) AND SKEWERS
These are useful for marbling chocolate and moving delicate shapes such as caraque or curls.

DECORATIVE CUTTERS
Small biscuit or aspic cutters are handy for making decorative shapes from thin sheets of set chocolate.

DOUBLE BOILER
This is useful for melting chocolate over simmering water, but a heatproof bowl fitted over an ordinary saucepan can be used instead, if done carefully.

FLEXIBLE SCRAPER
An asset when making chocolate caraque and shavings.

KNIVES
Small sharp knives are required for cutting chocolate shapes, while a large cook's knife with a rigid non-serrated blade is necessary for making caraque.

MARBLE SLAB
Although not essential, this provides a cold, flat surface for spreading chocolate to make caraque or shapes, and is also used when tempering chocolate. A clean work surface or an inverted baking sheet can be used instead.

MIXING BOWLS
Mixing bowls in various sizes are essential. Heatproof bowls are necessary for melting chocolate, and a large glass or ceramic bowl will be invaluable for whisking egg whites.

PAINTBRUSHES
Small paintbrushes can be used for spreading chocolate thinly over leaves or inside moulds. Choose good quality brushes which will not shed hairs.

PALETTE KNIFE
This is the perfect tool for spreading melted chocolate or frostings.

SIEVE
A standard sieve is needed for sifting cocoa and icing sugar. For very small quantities, use a tea strainer.

VEGETABLE PEELER
Use this for making chocolate curls.

1. DOUBLE BOILER

2. KNIFE

3. PALETTE KNIFE

4. FLEXIBLE SCRAPER

5. CHEESE SLICER

6. VEGETABLE PEELER

7. CHOCOLATE TOOLS

8. CHOCOLATE/CANDY THERMOMETER

9. PAINTBRUSHES

10. COCKTAIL STICKS (TOOTHPICKS)

11. CHOCOLATE MOULDS

12. COOKIE CUTTERS

13. SIEVE

14. MIXING BOWLS

15. MARBLE SLAB

$\mathcal{S}$MALL CAKES AND BAKES

There's no end to the ways to use chocolate in
small cakes and cookies. Start the day with a
warm Brioche au Chocolat for breakfast,
or treat yourself at coffee time with rich,
totally indulgent Nut and Chocolate Chip
Brownies or Double Chocolate Chip Muffins.
Or, if you're after an elegant touch of texture
to serve alongside a creamy dinner party
dessert, light, crisp Chocolate Cinnamon
Tuiles are the perfect choice.

Nut and Chocolate Chip Brownies

150g/5oz dark (unsweetened) chocolate, broken into squares

120ml/4fl oz/½ cup sunflower oil

215g/7½oz/1¼ cups light muscovado (light brown) sugar

2 eggs

5ml/1 tsp vanilla extract

65g/2½oz/⅔ cup self-rising flour

60ml/4 tbsp cocoa powder

75g/3oz/¾ cup chopped walnuts or pecan nuts

60ml/4 tbsp milk chocolate chips

⌒ MAKES 16 ⌒

> *Moist, dark and deeply satisfying –*
> *meet the ultimate chocolate brownie.*

1 Preheat the oven to
~ 180°C/350°F/Gas 4.
Butter a shallow 19cm/7½in
square cake tin. Melt the
dark chocolate in a heat-
proof bowl over hot water.

COOK'S TIP

*These brownies will
freeze for 3 months in an
airtight container*

2 Beat the oil, sugar, eggs
~ and vanilla extract
together in a large bowl.

3 Stir in the melted
~ chocolate, then beat well
until evenly mixed.

4 Sift the flour and cocoa
~ powder into the bowl
and fold in thoroughly.

5 Stir in the chopped nuts
~ and chocolate chips, tip
into the prepared tin and
spread evenly to the edges.

6 Bake for 30-35 minutes,
~ or until the top is firm
and crusty. Cool in the tin
before cutting into squares.

WHITE CHOCOLATE MACADAMIA SLICES

INGREDIENTS

150g/5oz/1¼ cups macadamia nuts, blanched almonds or hazelnuts

400g/14oz white chocolate, broken into squares

50g/2oz/½ cup ready-to-eat dried apricots

75g/3oz/6 tbsp unsalted butter

5ml/1 tsp vanilla extract

3 eggs

150g/5oz/scant 1 cup light muscovado (light brown) sugar

115g/4oz/1 cup self-rising flour

~ MAKES 16 ~

Keep these luxury slices for someone special who'll really appreciate their superb rich flavour and crunchy texture.

1 Preheat the oven to 190°C/375°F/Gas 5. Lightly grease two 20cm/8in round sandwich cake tins and line the base of each with baking parchment.

2 Roughly chop the nuts and half the white chocolate, making sure that the pieces are more or less the same size. Then cut the apricots in similar size pieces.

3 In the top of a double boiler or a heatproof bowl over simmering water, melt the remaining white chocolate with the butter. Remove from the heat and stir in the vanilla extract.

4 Whisk the eggs and sugar together in a mixing bowl until thick and pale, then whisk in the melted chocolate mixture.

5 Sift the flour over the mixture and fold it in evenly. Stir in the nuts, chopped white chocolate and chopped dried apricots.

6 Spoon into the tin and level the top. Bake for 30-35 minutes, or until the top is firm and crusty. Cool in the tin before slicing.

COOK'S TIP

Use kitchen scissors to snip the apricots into small pieces.

CHOCOLATE CINNAMON TUILES

Slim, curvy and quite irresistible, tuiles are the perfect accompaniment for sophisticated desserts.

INGREDIENTS

1 egg white

50g/2oz/¼ cup caster (superfine) sugar

30ml/2 tbsp plain (all-purpose) flour

40g/1½oz/3 tbsp butter, melted

15ml/1 tbsp cocoa powder

2.5ml/½ tsp ground cinnamon

~ MAKES 12 ~

1 Preheat the oven to ~ 200°C/400°F/Gas 6. Lightly grease two large baking sheets. Whisk the egg white in a clean, grease-free bowl until it forms soft peaks. Gradually whisk in the sugar to make a smooth, glossy mixture.

COOK'S TIP

Work as quickly as possible when removing the tuiles from the baking sheets – if they firm up too quickly, pop the baking sheet back in the oven for a minute and try again.

2 Sift the flour over the ~ mixture and fold in evenly. Stir in the butter. Transfer about 45ml/3 tbsp of the mixture to a small bowl and set it aside.

3 In a separate bowl, mix ~ together the cocoa and cinnamon. Stir into the larger quantity of mixture.

4 Leaving room for ~ spreading, drop spoonfuls of the chocolate-flavoured mixture on to the prepared baking sheets, then spread each gently with a metal frosting knife to make a neat round.

5 Using a small spoon, ~ drizzle the reserved plain mixture over the rounds, swirling it lightly to give a marbled effect.

6 Bake for 4–6 minutes, ~ until just set. Using a palette knife, lift each biscuit and quickly drape it over a rolling pin, to give a curved shape as it hardens.

7 Allow the tuiles to cool ~ until set, then remove them gently and finish cooling on a wire rack. Serve on the same day.

DOUBLE CHOCOLATE CHIP MUFFINS

INGREDIENTS

400g/14oz/3½ cups plain (all-purpose) flour

15ml/1 tbsp baking powder

30ml/2 tbsp cocoa powder

115g/4oz/¾ cup dark muscovado (dark brown) sugar

2 eggs

150ml/¼ pint/⅔ cup soured cream

150ml/¼ pint/⅔ cup milk

60ml/4 tbsp sunflower oil

175g/6oz white chocolate

175g/6oz dark (semisweet) chocolate

cocoa powder, for dusting

MAKES 16

COOK'S TIP

If soured cream is not available, sour 150ml/ ¼ pint/⅔ cup single cream by stirring in 5ml/1 tsp lemon juice and letting the mixture stand until thickened.

Marvellous muffins, packed with lots of chunky dark and white chocolate chips.

1 Preheat the oven to 190°C/375°F/Gas 5. Place 16 paper muffin cases in muffin tins or deep patty tins. Sift the flour, baking powder and cocoa into a bowl and stir in the sugar. Make a well in the centre.

2 In a separate bowl, beat the eggs with the soured cream, milk and oil, then stir into the well in the dry ingredients. Beat well, gradually incorporating the flour mixture to make a thick and creamy batter.

3 Chop both the white and the dark chocolate into small pieces, then stir into the batter mixture.

4 Spoon the mixture into the muffin cases, filling them almost to the top. Bake for 25–30 minutes, until well risen and firm to the touch. Cool on a wire rack, then dust with cocoa powder.

CHOCOLATE MARZIPAN COOKIES

INGREDIENTS

200g/7oz/scant 1 cup unsalted
butter, softened

200g/7oz/generous 1 cup light
muscovado (light brown) sugar

1 egg

300g/11oz/2¾ cups plain (all-purpose)
flour

60ml/4 tbsp cocoa powder

200g/7oz white almond paste

115g/4oz white chocolate,
broken into squares

MAKES ABOUT 36

Crisp little cookies for a sweet tooth, with a little almond surprise inside.

1 Preheat the oven to
~ 190°C/375°F/Gas 5.
Lightly grease two large
baking sheets. Cream the
butter with the sugar in a
bowl until pale and fluffy.
Add the egg and beat well.

2 Sift the flour and cocoa
~ over the mixture. Stir in,
first with a wooden spoon,
then with clean hands,
pressing the mixture
together to make a fairly
soft dough.

3 Roll out about half the
~ dough on a lightly
floured surface to a
thickness of about
5mm/¼in. Using a 5cm/2in
biscuit cutter, cut out
rounds, re-rolling the dough
as required until you have
about 36 rounds.

4 Cut the almond paste
~ into 36 equal pieces.
Roll into balls, flatten
slightly and place one on
each round of dough. Roll
out the remaining dough,
cut 36 rounds, then place
on top of the almond paste.
Press the edges to seal.

5 Bake for 10-12 minutes,
~ or until the cookies have
risen well and are beginning
to crack on the surface.
Leave on the baking sheet
for 2-3 minutes, then finish
cooling on a wire rack.

6 Melt the white
~ chocolate, then drizzle it
over the biscuits to
decorate, or use a paper
piping bag to pipe a design
on to the biscuits.

COOK'S TIP

*If the dough is too sticky
to roll, chill it for about
30 minutes, then
try again.*

$\mathcal{M}$OCHA VIENNESE SWIRLS

INGREDIENTS

115g/4oz dark (unsweetened) chocolate, broken into squares

200g/7oz/scant 1 cup unsalted butter, softened

50g/2oz/6 tbsp icing (confectioners') sugar

30ml/2 tbsp strong black coffee

200g/7oz/1¾ cups plain (all-purpose) flour

50g/2oz/½ cup cornflour (cornstarch)

To decorate

about 20 blanched almonds

150g/5oz dark (bittersweet) chocolate

~ MAKES ABOUT 20 ~

Some temptations just can't be resisted. Put out a plate of these melt-in-the-mouth marvels and watch them vanish.

3 Spoon the mixture into a piping bag fitted with a large star nozzle and pipe about 20 swirls on the baking sheets, allowing room for spreading during baking.

4 Press an almond into the centre of each swirl. Bake for about 15 minutes or until the biscuits are firm and just beginning to brown.

5 Leave to cool for about 10 minutes on the baking sheets, then lift carefully on to a wire rack to cool completely.

6 When cool, melt the chocolate and dip the base of each swirl to coat. Place on a sheet of baking parchment and leave to set.

1 Preheat the oven to 190°C/375°F/Gas 5. Lightly grease two large baking sheets. Melt the chocolate in a bowl over hot water. Cream the butter with the icing sugar in a bowl until smooth and pale. Beat in the melted chocolate, then the coffee.

2 Sift the flour and cornflour over the mixture. Fold in lightly and evenly to make a soft mixture.

$\mathcal{C}$OOK'S $\mathcal{T}$IP

If the mixture is too stiff to pipe, soften it with a little more black coffee.

CHUNKY DOUBLE CHOCOLATE COOKIES

Keep these luscious treats under lock and key unless you're feeling generous!

INGREDIENTS

115g/4oz/½ cup unsalted butter, softened

115g/4oz/⅔ cup light muscovado (light brown) sugar

1 egg

5ml/1 tsp vanilla extract

150g/5oz/1¼ cups self-rising flour

75g/3oz/¾ cup porridge (rolled) oats

115g/4oz dark (bittersweet) chocolate, roughly chopped

115g/4oz white chocolate, roughly chopped

MAKES 18–20

3 Mix in the oats and dark and white chocolate. Place small spoonfuls of the mixture in 18–20 rocky heaps on the baking sheets, leaving space for spreading.

4 Bake for 12-15 minutes or until the biscuits are beginning to turn pale golden. Cool for 2-3 minutes on the baking sheets, then lift on to wire racks to cool completely.

1 Preheat the oven to 190°C/375°F/Gas 5. Lightly grease two baking sheets. Cream the butter and sugar until pale and fluffy. Add the egg and vanilla extract and beat well.

2 Sift the flour over the butter and egg mixture and fold in lightly with a metal spoon.

COOK'S TIP

If you're short of time when making the cookies, substitute chocolate chips for the chopped chocolate. Chopped stem ginger would make a delicious addition as well.

CRANBERRY AND CHOCOLATE SQUARES

Made for each other — that's the contrasting flavours of tangy-sharp cranberries and sweet chocolate.

INGREDIENTS

150g/5oz/1¼ cups self-rising flour, plus extra for dusting

115g/4oz/½ cup unsalted butter

60ml/4 tbsp cocoa powder

215g/7½oz/1¼ cups light muscovado (light brown) sugar

2 eggs, beaten

115g/4oz/1⅓ cups fresh or thawed frozen cranberries

For the topping

150ml/¼ pint/⅔ cup soured cream

75g/3oz/6 tbsp caster (superfine) sugar

30ml/2 tbsp self-rising flour

50g/2oz/4 tbsp butter, softened

1 egg, beaten

2.5ml/½ tsp vanilla extract

75ml/5 tbsp coarsely grated dark chocolate for sprinkling

⯎ MAKES 12 ⯎

1 Preheat the oven to ∼ 180°C/350°F/Gas 4. Grease an 18 x 27cm/7 x 10½ in cake tin and dust lightly with flour. Combine the butter cocoa and sugar in a saucepan and stir over a low heat until melted and smooth.

2 Remove the melted ∼ mixture from the heat and stir in the flour and eggs, beating until mixed. Stir in the cranberries, then spread the mixture in the prepared tin.

3 Make the topping by ∼ mixing the ingredients in a bowl. Beat together, then spread over the base.

4 Sprinkle with the grated ∼ chocolate and bake for 40-45 minutes, until risen and firm. Cool in the tin, then cut into 12 squares.

CHOCOLATE CINNAMON DOUGHNUTS

Serve these light and luscious treats freshly made and just warm, so that the chocolate filling melts in your mouth.

INGREDIENTS

500g/1¼lb/5 cups strong (bread) flour

30ml/2 tbsp cocoa powder

2.5ml/½ tsp salt

1 sachet easy-blend dried yeast

300ml/½ pint/1¼ cups hand-hot milk

40g/1½oz/3 tbsp butter, melted

1 egg, beaten

115g/4oz dark (bittersweet) chocolate, broken into 16 pieces

sunflower oil for deep frying

For the coating

45ml/3 tbsp caster (superfine) sugar

15ml/1 tbsp cocoa powder

5ml/1 tsp ground cinnamon

MAKES 16

2 Knead the dough on a lightly floured surface for about 5 minutes, until smooth and elastic. Place in a clean bowl, cover and leave in a warm place until it has doubled in bulk.

3 Knead the dough lightly again, then divide into 16 pieces. Shape each into a round, press a piece of dark chocolate into the centre, then fold the dough over to enclose the filling, pressing firmly to make sure the edges are sealed. Re-shape the doughnuts when sealed, if necessary.

4 Heat the oil for deep frying to 180°C/350°F or until a cube of dried bread browns in 30-45 seconds. Deep fry the doughnuts in batches. As each one rises and turns golden brown, turn it over carefully to cook the other side. Drain the cooked doughnuts on kitchen paper.

5 Mix the sugar, cocoa and cinnamon in a shallow bowl. Toss the doughnuts in the mixture to coat them evenly. Serve warm or as soon as possible.

COOK'S TIP

If you are not planning to serve the doughnuts immediately, drain them on kitchen paper, cool completely and pack in a covered container. To serve, warm the doughnuts for a few minutes in a hot oven, then toss in the coating and serve warm.

1 Sift the flour, cocoa and salt into a large bowl. Stir in the yeast. Make a well in the centre and add the milk, melted butter and egg. Stir, to incorporate the dry ingredients and make a soft and pliable dough.

CHOCOLATE BUTTERSCOTCH BARS

INGREDIENTS

225g/8oz/2 cups plain (all-purpose) flour

2.5ml/½ tsp baking powder

115g/4oz/½ cup unsalted butter

50g/2oz/⅓ cup light muscovado (light brown) sugar

150g/5oz dark (unsweetened) chocolate, melted

30ml/2 tbsp ground almonds

For the topping

175g/6oz/¾ cup unsalted butter

115g/4oz/½ cup caster (superfine) sugar

30ml/2 tbsp golden (light corn) syrup

175ml/6fl oz/¾ cup condensed milk

150g/5oz/1¼ cups whole toasted hazelnuts

225g/8oz dark chocolate, broken into squares

MAKES 24

Unashamedly rich and sweet, these bars are perfect for chocoholics of all ages.

1 Preheat the oven to
~ 160°C/325°F/Gas 3.
Lightly grease a shallow 30 x 20cm/12 x 8in tin. Sift the flour and baking powder into a large bowl.

2 Rub in the butter until
~ the mixture resembles coarse breadcrumbs, then stir in the sugar. Work in the melted chocolate and ground almonds to make a light biscuit dough.

3 Press the dough evenly
~ into the prepared tin, prick the surface with a fork and bake for 25–30 minutes until firm. Leave to cool in the tin.

4 Make the topping. Mix
~ the butter, sugar, syrup and condensed milk in a pan. Heat gently, stirring, until the butter and sugar have melted. Simmer, stirring occasionally, until golden, then stir in the toasted hazelnuts.

5 Pour over the cooked
~ base. Leave to set.

6 Melt the chocolate in a
~ heatproof bowl over hot water. Spread evenly over the butterscotch layer, then leave to set again before cutting into bars to serve.

B RIOCHES AU CHOCOLAT

Steal out of bed early and surprise the one you love with these wonderful French specialities. Light, golden and drizzled with melted chocolate, they are bound to go down well.

INGREDIENTS

250g/9oz/2¼ cups strong (bread) flour

pinch of salt

30ml/2 tbsp caster (superfine) sugar

1 sachet easy-blend dried yeast

3 eggs, beaten, plus extra beaten egg, for glazing

45ml/3 tbsp hand-hot milk

115g/4oz/½ cup unsalted butter, diced

150g/5oz dark (semisweet) chocolate, broken into squares

MAKES 12

1 Sift the flour, salt and sugar into a large bowl and stir in the yeast. Make a well in the centre of the mixture and add the eggs and milk.

2 Beat well, gradually incorporating the surrounding dry ingredients to make a fairly soft dough. Turn on to a lightly floured surface and knead well until smooth and elastic, adding a little more flour if necessary.

3 Add the butter to the dough, a few pieces at a time, kneading until each addition is absorbed before adding the next. When all the butter has been incorporated and small bubbles appear in the dough, wrap it and chill for at least 1 hour, or overnight.

4 Lightly grease 12 brioche tins set on a baking sheet or a 12-hole brioche or muffin tin. Divide the dough into 12 and shape each into a ball. Place a chocolate square in the centre. Bring up the sides of the dough and press the edges firmly together to seal.

5 Place the brioches, join side down, in the tins. Cover and leave them in a warm place for about 30 minutes or until doubled in size. Preheat the oven to 200°C/400°F/Gas 6.

6 Brush with beaten egg; bake for 12-15 minutes, until well risen and golden brown. Place on wire racks. Melt the remaining chocolate and drizzle it over the brioches. Serve warm.

$\mathcal{L}$ARGE CAKES, LOAVES AND PIES

There can be few families who wouldn't leap enthusiastically upon a simple chocolate sponge cake, so think how they'll drool at the sight of a deep, sticky slice of Chocolate Pecan Pie, or Frosted Chocolate Fudge Cake. If cheesecakes are a family favourite, try Baked Chocolate and Raisin Cheesecake – so simple to make and well worth it for all the praise you'll get!

CHOCOLATE PECAN PIE

If you thought pecan pie couldn't be improved upon, just try this gorgeous chocolate one with its rich orange crust.

INGREDIENTS

200g/7oz/1¾ cups plain (all-purpose) flour

65g/2½oz/5 tbsp caster (superfine) sugar

90g/3½oz/scant ½ cup unsalted butter, softened

1 egg, beaten

finely grated rind of 1 orange

For the filling

200g/7oz/¾ cup golden (light corn) syrup

45ml/3 tbsp light muscovado (light brown) sugar

150g/5oz dark (unsweetened) chocolate, broken into squares

50g/2oz/4 tbsp butter

3 eggs, beaten

5ml/1 tsp vanilla extract

175g/6oz/1½ cups pecan nuts

~ SERVES 6 ~

1 Sift the flour into a bowl
~ and stir in the sugar.
Work in the butter with the
fingertips until combined.

2 Beat the egg and orange
~ rind in a bowl, then stir
into the mixture to make a
firm dough. Add a little
water if the mixture seems
too dry.

3 Roll out the pastry on a
~ lightly floured surface
and use to line a deep,
20cm/8in loose-based flan
tin. Chill for 30 minutes.

4 Preheat the oven to
~ 180°C/350°F/Gas 4.
Make the filling. Mix the
syrup, sugar, chocolate and
butter in a small saucepan.
Heat gently until melted.

5 Remove from the heat
~ and beat in the eggs and
vanilla extract. Sprinkle the
pecan nuts into the pastry
case and carefully pour over
the chocolate mixture.

6 Place on a baking sheet
~ and bake for 50-60
minutes or until set. Cool in
the tin.

COOK'S TIP

*Make individual tartlets
if you prefer – use six
10cm/4in flan (tartlet)
tins and bake at the
same temperature for
about 30 minutes.
Walnuts or almonds can
be used instead of pecans.*

FROSTED CHOCOLATE FUDGE CAKE

Rich and dreamy, with an irresistible chocolate fudgy frosting, this cake couldn't be easier to make, or more wonderful to eat!

INGREDIENTS

115g/4oz dark (unsweetened) chocolate, broken into squares

175g/6oz/¾ cup unsalted butter, softened

200g/7oz/generous 1 cup light muscovado (light brown) sugar

5ml/1 tsp vanilla extract

3 eggs, beaten

150ml/¼ pint/⅔ cup Greek-style (US strained, plain) yogurt

150g/5oz/1¼ cups self-rising flour

icing (confectioners') sugar and chocolate curls, to decorate

For the frosting

115g/4oz dark (bittersweet) chocolate, broken into squares

50g/2oz/4 tbsp unsalted butter

350g/12oz/3 cups icing (confectioners') sugar

90ml/6 tbsp Greek-style (US strained, plain) yogurt

⁓ SERVES 6–8 ⁓

COOK'S TIP

If the frosting begins to set too quickly, heat it gently to soften, and beat in a little extra yogurt if necessary.

1 Preheat the oven to 190°C/375°F/Gas 5. Grease two 20cm/8in round sandwich cake tins and line the base of each with non-stick baking paper. Melt the chocolate in a heatproof bowl over hot water.

2 In a mixing bowl, cream the butter or margarine with the sugar until light and fluffy. Beat in the vanilla extract, then gradually add the beaten eggs, beating well after each addition.

3 Stir in the melted dark chocolate and yogurt evenly. Fold in the flour with a metal spoon.

4 Divide the mixture between the prepared tins. Bake for 25–30 minutes or until the cakes are firm. Turn out and cool on a wire rack.

5 Make the frosting. Melt the chocolate and butter in a saucepan over a low heat. Remove from the heat and stir in the icing sugar and yogurt. Mix with a rubber spatula until smooth, then beat until the frosting cools and thickens slightly. Use a third of the mixture to sandwich the cakes.

6 Working quickly, spread the remainder over the top and sides. Sprinkle with icing sugar and decorate with chocolate curls.

CHOCOLATE GINGER CRUNCH CAKE

INGREDIENTS

150g/5oz dark (bittersweet) chocolate, broken into squares

50g/2oz/4 tbsp unsalted butter

115g/4oz ginger cookies

4 pieces preserved stem ginger

30ml/2 tbsp stem ginger syrup

45ml/3 tbsp desiccated (unsweetened shredded) coconut

To decorate

25g/1oz milk chocolate

pieces of crystallized ginger

SERVES 6

Ginger adds a flicker of fire to this delectable uncooked cake. Keep one in the fridge for midnight feasts and other late-night treats.

1 Grease a 15cm/6in flan ring; place it on a sheet of non-stick baking paper. Melt the chocolate with the butter in a heatproof bowl over barely simmering water. Remove from the heat.

3 Chop the stem ginger fairly finely and mix with the crushed cookies.

5 Tip the mixture into the prepared flan ring and press down firmly and evenly. Chill until set.

2 Crush the cookies into small pieces (see Cook's Tip). Tip them into a bowl.

4 Stir the biscuit mixture, ginger syrup and coconut into the melted chocolate and butter, mixing well until evenly combined.

6 Remove the flan ring and slide the cake on to a plate. Melt the milk chocolate, drizzle it over the top and decorate with the pieces of crystallized ginger.

COOK'S TIP

Do not crush the cookies completely, as you need some larger pieces for texture. Place in a thick plastic bag and hit with a rolling pin, or pulse in a food processor, for greater control.

BAKED CHOCOLATE AND RAISIN CHEESECAKE

If you just can't get enough chocolate, this delectable cheesecake will be your idea of heaven. Its crisp chocolate shortbread base is covered with a creamy chocolate chip filling, topped off with a sticky chocolate glaze.

INGREDIENTS

75g/3oz/¾ cup plain (all-purpose) flour

45ml/3 tbsp cocoa powder

75g/3oz/½ cup semolina

50g/2oz/¼ cup caster (superfine) sugar

115g/4oz/½ cup unsalted butter, softened

For the filling

225g/8oz/1 cup cream cheese

120ml/4fl oz/½ cup natural (plain) yogurt

2 eggs, beaten

75g/3oz/6 tbsp caster (superfine) sugar

finely grated zest of 1 lemon

75g/3oz/½ cup raisins

45ml/3 tbsp dark (semisweet) chocolate chips

For the topping

75g/3oz dark (unsweetened) chocolate, broken into squares

30ml/2 tbsp golden (light corn) syrup

40g/1½oz/3 tbsp butter

≈ SERVES 8–10 ≈

1 Preheat the oven to 150°C/300°F/Gas 2. Sift the flour and cocoa into a mixing bowl with the semolina and sugar. Work the butter into the flour mixture with your fingers until it makes a firm dough.

2 Press the dough into the base of a 22cm/8½ in springform tin. Prick with a fork and bake in the oven for 15 minutes. Remove the tin from the oven.

3 In a large bowl, beat the cream cheese with the yogurt, eggs and sugar until evenly mixed. Stir in the lemon zest, raisins and chocolate chips.

> ### COOK'S TIP
>
> *For a slightly quicker version, omit the topping and simply drizzle melted chocolate over the cheesecake to finish.*

4 Smooth the cream cheese mixture over the base and bake for a further 35-45 minutes, or until the filling is pale gold and just set. Cool in the tin.

5 For the topping, place the chocolate, syrup and butter in a heatproof bowl. Set over a pan of simmering water and heat, stirring occasionally, until melted. Pour over the cheesecake and leave to cool until set.

CHOCOLATE CHIP MARZIPAN LOAF

INGREDIENTS

115g/4oz/½ cup unsalted butter, softened

150g/5oz/scant 1 cup light muscovado (light brown) sugar

2 eggs

45ml/3 tbsp cocoa powder

150g/5oz/1¼ cups self-rising flour

130g/4½oz marzipan

60ml/4 tbsp dark (semisweet) chocolate chips

MAKES 1 LOAF

Sometimes plain wrappers disguise the most marvellous surprises. Inside this ordinary-looking loaf are creamy chunks of marzipan and chips of chocolate.

1 Preheat the oven to
~ 180°C/350°F/Gas 4.
Grease a 900g/2lb loaf tin
and line the base with
baking parchment. Cream
the butter and sugar in a
bowl until light and fluffy.

2 Add the eggs to the
~ creamed mixture one at
a time, beating well after
each addition to combine.

3 Sift the cocoa and flour
~ over the mixture and
fold in evenly.

4 Chop the marzipan into
~ small pieces with a sharp
knife. Tip into a bowl and
mix with the chocolate
chips. Set aside about
60ml/4 tbsp and fold the
rest evenly into the cake
mixture.

5 Scrape the mixture into
~ the prepared tin, level the
top and scatter with the
reserved marzipan and
chocolate chips.

6 Bake for 45–50 minutes
~ or until the loaf is risen
and firm. Cool for a few
minutes in the tin, then
turn out on to a wire rack
to cool completely.

COOK'S TIP

This cake is ideal for freezing, either whole or in handy slices separated by sheets of plastic wrap. Wrap it in foil and freeze for up to 3 months.

$\mathscr{S}$TICKY CHOCOLATE, MAPLE AND WALNUT SWIRLS

INGREDIENTS

450g/1lb/4 cups strong (bread) flour

2.5ml/½ tsp ground cinnamon

50g/2oz/4 tbsp unsalted butter

50g/2oz/¼ cup caster (superfine) sugar

1 sachet easy-blend dried yeast

1 egg yolk

120ml/4fl oz/½ cup water

60ml/4 tbsp milk

45ml/3 tbsp maple syrup, to finish

For the filling

40g/1½oz/3 tbsp unsalted butter, melted

50g/2oz/⅓ cup light muscovado (light brown) sugar

175g/6oz/1 cup dark (semisweet) chocolate chips

75g/3oz/¾ cup chopped walnuts

SERVES 12

This rich yeasted cake breaks into separate sticky chocolate swirls, each soaked in maple syrup.

1 Grease a deep 23cm/9in springform cake tin. Sift the flour and cinnamon into a bowl, then rub in the butter until the mixture resembles coarse breadcrumbs.

2 Stir in the sugar and yeast. In a jug or bowl, beat the egg yolk with the water and milk, then stir into the dry ingredients to make a soft dough (see Cook's Tip).

3 Knead the dough on a lightly floured surface until smooth, then roll out to a rectangle measuring about 40 x 30cm/16 x 12in.

4 Brush the dough with the melted butter. Sprinkle the sugar, chocolate chips and nuts on top.

5 Roll up the dough from one long side like a Swiss roll, then cut into 12 thick even-size slices.

6 Pack the slices closely together in the prepared tin, with the cut sides facing upwards. Cover and leave in a warm place for about 1½ hours, until well risen and springy to the touch. Preheat the oven to 220°C/425°F/Gas 7.

7 Bake the swirls for about 30-35 minutes until well risen, golden brown and firm. Remove from the tin and cool on a wire rack. To finish, spoon or brush the maple syrup over the cake. Pull the pieces apart to serve.

$\mathscr{C}$OOK'S $\mathscr{T}$IP

The amount of liquid added to the dry ingredients may have to be adjusted slightly as some flours absorb more liquid than others. The dough should be soft but not sticky.

BITTER MARMALADE CHOCOLATE LOAF

INGREDIENTS

115g/4oz dark (unsweetened) chocolate, broken into squares

3 eggs

200g/7oz/scant 1 cup caster (superfine) sugar

175ml/6fl oz/¾ cup soured cream

200g/7oz/1¾ cups self-rising flour

For the filling and glaze

175g/6oz/⅔ cup bitter orange marmalade

115g/4oz dark (semisweet) chocolate, broken into squares

60ml/4 tbsp soured cream

shredded orange rind, to decorate

☞ SERVES 8 ☜

Don't be alarmed at the amount of cream in this recipe — it's naughty but necessary, and replaces butter to make a moist dark cake, topped with a bitter-sweet sticky marmalade topping.

1 Preheat the oven to
~ 180°C/350°F/Gas 4.
Grease a 900g/2lb loaf tin lightly, then line it with baking parchment. Melt the chocolate in a heatproof bowl over hot water.

2 Combine the eggs and
~ sugar in a separate bowl. Using a hand-held electric mixer, whisk the mixture until it is thick and creamy, then stir in the soured cream and chocolate. Fold in the self-rising flour.

3 Scrape the mixture into
~ the prepared tin and bake for about 1 hour or until well risen and firm to the touch. Cool for a few minutes in the tin, then turn on to a wire rack and leave to cool completely.

4 Make the filling. Spoon
~ two-thirds of the marmalade into a small pan and melt over a gentle heat. Melt the chocolate and stir it into the marmalade with the soured cream.

5 Slice the cake across into
~ three layers and sandwich back together with about half the marmalade filling. Spread the rest over the top of the cake and leave to set. Spoon the remaining marmalade over the cake and scatter with shredded orange rind, to decorate.

COOK'S TIP

If you don't particularly like marmalade, use apricot jam instead.

CHOCOLATE AND CHERRY POLENTA CAKE

INGREDIENTS

50g/2oz/⅓ cup quick-cook polenta

200g/7oz dark (unsweetened) chocolate, broken into squares

5 eggs, separated

175g/6oz/¾ cup caster (superfine) sugar

115g/4oz/1 cup ground almonds

60ml/4 tbsp plain (all-purpose) flour

finely grated zest of 1 orange

115g/4oz/½ cup glacé (candied) cherries, halved

icing (confectioners') sugar, for dusting

SERVES 8

Perfect for packing to take on a romantic picnic, this chocolate cherry cake is dense and delicious. Polenta and almonds add an unusual nutty texture.

3 Whisk the egg yolks
~ with the sugar in a large bowl until thick and pale. Beat in the melted chocolate, then fold in the polenta, ground almonds, flour and orange zest.

4 Whisk the egg whites in
~ a clean, grease-free bowl until stiff. Stir about 15ml/ 1 tbsp of the whites into the chocolate mixture to lighten it, then fold in the rest. Finally, fold in the cherries.

1 Place the polenta in a
~ heatproof bowl and pour over boiling water to cover; about 120ml/4fl oz/½ cup. Stir well, then cover the bowl and leave to stand for about 30 minutes, until the polenta has absorbed all the excess moisture.

COOK'S TIP

It is important to add only just enough water to cover the polenta, as too much moisture in the mixture will cause the cherries to sink. If necessary, drain off excess moisture.

5 Scrape the mixture into
~ the prepared tin and bake for 45-55 minutes or until well risen and firm to the touch. Turn out and cool on a wire rack, then dust with icing sugar to serve.

2 Preheat the oven to
~ 190°C/375°F/Gas 5. Grease a deep 22cm/8½in round cake tin and line the base with baking parchment. Melt the chocolate in a bowl over hot water.

MARBLED SWISS ROLL

WITH CHOCOLATE AND WALNUT BUTTERCREAM

90g/3½oz/scant 1 cup plain (all-purpose) flour

15ml/1 tbsp cocoa powder

25g/1oz dark (semisweet) chocolate, grated

25g/1oz white chocolate, grated

3 eggs

115g/4oz/½ cup caster (superfine) sugar

30ml/2 tbsp boiling water

For the filling

1 quantity Chocolate Buttercream

45ml/3 tbsp chopped walnuts

SERVES 6–8

Simply sensational – that's the combination of light chocolate sponge and walnut chocolate buttercream.

1 Preheat the oven to 200°C/400°F/Gas 6. Grease and line a 30 x 20cm/12 x 8in Swiss roll tin. Sift half the flour with the cocoa into bowl. Stir in the grated dark chocolate. Sift the remaining flour into another bowl and add the grated white chocolate.

2 Whisk the eggs and sugar in a heatproof bowl over a pan of hot water until it holds its shape.

3 Remove the bowl from the heat and tip half the mixture into a clean bowl. Fold the white chocolate mixture into one portion, then fold the dark chocolate mixture into the other. Stir 15ml/1 tbsp boiling water into each half to soften the mixtures.

4 Place alternate spoonfuls of mixture in the prepared tin and swirl lightly together for to marble. Bake for about 12-15 minutes, or until firm. Turn out on to a sheet of baking parchment.

5 Trim the edges to neaten and cover with a damp, clean dish towel.

6 For the filling, mix the buttercream and walnuts in a bowl. When the sponge is completely cold, uncover, lift off the lining paper and spread the surface with the buttercream. Roll up carefully from a long side and place on a serving plate. Decorate with dark and white chocolate curls.

COOK'S TIP

Use a skewer to swirl the chocolate and plain mixtures together.

SIMPLE CHOCOLATE CAKE

An easy, everyday chocolate cake which can be simply filled with buttercream, or pepped up with a rich chocolate ganache for a special occasion.

INGREDIENTS

115g/4oz dark (semisweet) chocolate, broken into squares
45ml/3 tbsp milk
150g/5oz/⅔ cup unsalted butter, softened
150g/5oz/scant 1 cup light muscovado (light brown) sugar
3 eggs
200g/7oz/1¾ cups self-rising flour
15ml/1 tbsp cocoa powder
1 quantity Chocolate Buttercream
icing (confectioners') sugar and cocoa powder, for dusting

SERVES 6–8

1 Preheat the oven to 180°C/350°F/Gas 4. Grease two 18cm/7in round sandwich cake tins and line the bases with baking parchment. Melt the chocolate with the milk in a heatproof bowl set over a pan of simmering water.

2 Cream the butter with the sugar in a mixing bowl until pale and fluffy. Add the eggs one at a time, beating well after each addition. Stir in the chocolate mixture until well combined.

COOK'S TIP

For a richer finish, make a double quantity of buttercream and spread or pipe over the top of the cake as well as using for the filling.

3 Sift the flour and cocoa over the mixture and fold in with a metal spoon until evenly mixed. Scrape into the prepared tins, smooth level and bake for 35–40 minutes or until well risen and firm. Turn out on wire racks to cool.

4 Sandwich the cake layers together with the buttercream. Dust with a mixture of icing sugar and cocoa just before serving.

SPECIAL OCCASION CAKES

*Any special celebration is a good excuse for
indulgence and nothing could be more
indulgent than a luxuriously rich chocolate
gâteau or a lavish Sachertorte, or try out your
skills on a more unusual, impressive Rich
Chocolate Leaf Gâteau. Alternatively, you
could disregard everyone's diet and go totally
overboard with the richest chocolate cake ever
– Death by Chocolate!*

SACHERTORTE

Rich and dark, with a wonderful flavour, this glorious gâteau was created in Vienna in 1832 by Franz Sacher, a chef in the royal household.

INGREDIENTS

225g/8oz dark (bittersweet) chocolate, broken into squares

150g/5oz/⅔ cup unsalted butter, softened

115g/4oz/½ cup caster (superfine) sugar

8 eggs, separated

115g/4oz/1 cup plain (all-purpose) flour

For the glaze

225g/8oz/1 cup apricot jam

15ml/1 tbsp lemon juice

For the icing

225g/8oz dark (bittersweet) chocolate, broken into squares

200g/7oz/scant 1 cup caster (superfine) sugar

15ml/1 tbsp golden (light corn) syrup

250ml/8fl oz/1 cup double (heavy) cream

5ml/1 tsp vanilla extract

dark (bittersweet) chocolate curls, to decorate

◆ SERVES 10–12 ◆

1 Preheat the oven to
~ 180°C/350°F/Gas 4.
Grease a 23cm/9in round springform cake tin and line with baking parchment.

2 Melt the chocolate in a
~ heatproof bowl over hot water. Cream the butter with the sugar in a mixing bowl until pale and fluffy, then add the egg yolks, one at a time, beating after each addition. Beat in the melted chocolate, then sift the flour over the mixture and fold it in evenly.

3 Whisk the egg whites in
~ a clean, grease-free bowl until stiff, then stir about a quarter of the whites into the chocolate mixture to lighten it. Fold in the remaining whites.

4 Tip the mixture into the
~ prepared cake tin and smooth level. Bake for about 50-55 minutes, or until firm. Turn out on to a wire rack to cool.

5 Make the glaze. Heat
~ the apricot jam with the lemon juice in a small saucepan until melted, then strain into a bowl. Once the cake is cold, slice in half across the middle to make two even-size layers.

6 Brush the top and sides
~ of each layer with the apricot glaze, then sandwich them together. Place on a wire rack.

7 Make the icing. Mix the
~ chocolate, sugar, syrup, cream and vanilla extract in a heavy saucepan. Heat gently, stirring constantly, until the mixture is thick and smooth. Simmer gently for 3-4 minutes, without stirring, until the mixture registers 95°C/200°F on a chocolate or candy thermometer.

8 Pour the icing quickly
~ over the cake, spreading to cover the top and sides completely. Leave to set, decorate with chocolate curls, then serve with whipped cream if wished.

COOK'S TIP

Use the finest dark chocolate you can afford to make this gâteau — the expense will be amply justified.

WHITE CHOCOLATE CAPPUCCINO GATEAU

4 eggs
115g/4oz/½ cup caster (superfine) sugar
15ml/1 tbsp strong black coffee
2.5ml/½ tsp vanilla extract
115g/4oz/1 cup plain (all-purpose) flour
75g/3oz white chocolate, coarsely grated
For the filling
120ml/4fl oz/½ cup double (heavy) cream
15ml/1 tbsp coffee liqueur
For the frosting and topping
15ml/1 tbsp coffee liqueur
1 quantity White Chocolate Frosting
white chocolate curls
cocoa powder or powdered cinnamon, for dusting

SERVES 8

COOK'S TIP

If you don't have any coffee liqueur, use brandy or dark rum instead. For an alcohol-free version, substitute strong black coffee.

Luscious, lavish and laced with liqueur, this is strictly for adults only!

1 Preheat the oven to
~ 180°C/350°F/Gas 4.
Grease two 19cm/7½in
round sandwich cake tins
and line the base of each
with baking parchment.

2 Combine the eggs,
~ caster sugar, coffee and
vanilla extract in a large
heatproof bowl. Place over a
saucepan of hot water and
whisk until pale and thick
enough to hold its shape
when the whisk is lifted.

3 Sift half the flour over
~ the mixture; fold in
gently and evenly. Fold in
the remaining flour with the
grated white chocolate.

4 Divide the mixture
~ between the prepared
tins and smooth level. Bake
for 20-25 minutes, until
firm and golden, then turn
out on wire racks and leave
to cool completely.

5 Make the filling. Whip
~ the cream with the
coffee liqueur in a bowl
until it holds its shape.
Spread over one of the
cakes, then place the second
layer on top.

6 Stir the coffee liqueur
~ into the frosting. Spread
over the top and sides of the
cake, swirling with a palette
knife. Top with curls of
white chocolate and dust
with cocoa or cinnamon.

CHOCOLATE REDCURRANT TORTE

Redcurrants are perfect partners for chocolate in this glossy gâteau, as their slightly sharp-sweet flavour balances the rich chocolate beautifully.

INGREDIENTS

115g/4oz/½ cup unsalted butter, softened

115g/4oz/⅔ cup dark muscovado (dark brown) sugar

2 eggs

150ml/¼ pint/⅔ cup soured cream

150g/5oz/1¼ cups self-rising flour

5ml/1 tsp baking powder

45ml/3 tbsp cocoa powder

75g/3oz/¾ cup stemmed redcurrants, plus 115g/4oz/1 cup redcurrant sprigs, to decorate

For the icing

150g/5oz dark (bittersweet) chocolate, broken into squares

45ml/3 tbsp redcurrant jelly

30ml/2 tbsp dark rum

120ml/4fl oz/½ cup double (heavy) cream

 SERVES 8–10

COOK'S TIP

If redcurrants are not available, use other small soft fruits such as raspberries or blackcurrants instead.

1 Preheat the oven to ~ 180°C/350°F/Gas 4. Grease a 1.2 litre/2 pint/ 5 cup ring tin and dust lightly with flour. Cream the butter with the sugar in a mixing bowl until pale and fluffy. Beat in the eggs and soured cream until thoroughly mixed.

2 Sift the flour, baking ~ powder and cocoa over the mixture, then fold in lightly and evenly. Fold in the stemmed redcurrants.

3 Spoon the mixture into ~ the prepared tin and smooth the surface level. Bake for 40-50 minutes or until well risen and firm. Turn out on to a wire rack and leave to cool completely.

4 Make the icing. Mix the ~ chocolate, redcurrant jelly and rum in a heatproof bowl. Set the bowl over simmering water and heat gently, stirring occasionally, until melted. Remove the bowl from the heat and stir in the cream.

5 Transfer the cooked cake ~ to a serving plate. Spoon the icing evenly over the cake, allowing it to drizzle down the sides. Decorate with redcurrant sprigs just before serving.

CHOCOLATE ALMOND MOUSSE CAKE

INGREDIENTS

50g/2oz dark (bittersweet) chocolate, broken into squares

200g/7oz marzipan, grated or chopped

200ml/7fl oz/scant 1 cup milk

115g/4oz/1 cup self-rising flour

2 eggs, separated

75g/3oz/½ cup light muscovado (light brown) sugar

For the mousse filling

115g/4oz dark (bittersweet) chocolate, broken into squares

50g/2oz/4 tbsp unsalted butter

2 eggs, separated

30ml/2 tbsp Amaretto di Saronno liqueur

For the topping

1 quantity Chocolate Ganache

toasted flaked almonds, to decorate

⌁ SERVES 8 ⌁

Surrender to a taste sensation with this superb combination of chocolate and almonds.

1 Preheat the oven to
~ 190°C/375°F/Gas 5.
Grease a deep 17cm/6½in square cake tin and line with baking parchment. Combine the chocolate, marzipan and milk in a saucepan and heat gently without boiling, stirring until melted and smooth.

2 Sift the flour into a bowl
~ and add the chocolate mixture and egg yolks, beating until evenly mixed.

COOK'S TIP

It is important that the chocolate mixture is hot when you beat in the yolks, so that they cook slightly.

3 Whisk the egg whites in
~ a clean, grease-free bowl until stiff enough to hold firm peaks. Whisk in the sugar gradually. Stir about 15ml/1 tbsp of the whites into the chocolate mixture to lighten it, then fold in the rest.

4 Spoon the mixture into
~ the tin, spreading it evenly. Bake for 45–50 minutes, until well risen, firm and springy to the touch. Leave to cool on a wire rack.

5 Make the mousse filling.
~ Melt the chocolate with the butter in a heatproof bowl over barely simmering water, then remove from the heat and beat in the egg yolks and Amaretto. Whisk the egg whites in a clean, grease-free bowl until stiff, then fold into the chocolate mixture.

6 Slice the cold cake in
~ half across the middle to make two even layers. Return one half to the clean cake tin and pour over the chocolate mousse. Top with the second layer of cake and press down lightly. Chill until set.

7 Turn the cake out on to
~ a serving plate. Spread the chocolate ganache over the top and sides, then press toasted, flaked almonds over the sides. Serve chilled.

DEATH BY CHOCOLATE

INGREDIENTS

225g/8oz dark (bittersweet) chocolate, broken into squares

115g/4oz/½ cup unsalted butter

150ml/¼ pint/⅔ cup milk

225g/8oz/1¼ cups light muscovado (light brown) sugar

10ml/2 tsp vanilla extract

2 eggs, separated

150ml/¼ pint/⅔ cup soured cream

225g/8oz/2 cups self-rising flour

5ml/1 tsp baking powder

For the filling and topping

60ml/4 tbsp seedless raspberry jam

60ml/4 tbsp brandy

400g/14oz dark (bittersweet) chocolate, broken into squares

200g/7oz/scant 1 cup unsalted butter

1 quantity Chocolate Ganache

chocolate curls, and physalis (Cape gooseberries), to decorate

SERVES 16–20

One of the richest chocolate cakes ever, this should be served in thin slices. True chocoholics can always come back for more!

1 Preheat the oven to
~ 180°C/350°F/Gas 4.
Grease and base-line a deep 23cm/9in springform cake tin. Place the chocolate, butter and milk in a pan. Melt over a low heat until smooth. Remove from the heat, beat in the sugar and vanilla and set aside.

2 Beat the egg yolks and
~ cream in a bowl, then beat into the chocolate mixture. Sift and fold in the flour and baking powder.

3 Whisk the egg whites in
~ a grease-free bowl until stiff; fold into the mixture.

4 Scrape into the prepared
~ tin and bake for about 45–55 minutes, or until firm to the touch. Cool in the tin for 15 minutes, then invert on a rack to cool.

5 Slice the cake across the
~ middle to make three layers. In a small saucepan, warm the jam with 15ml/ 1 tbsp of the brandy, then brush over two of the layers; leave to set. Place the remaining brandy in a saucepan with the chocolate and butter. Heat gently, stirring, until smooth. Cool until beginning to thicken.

6 Spread the bottom layer
~ of the cake with half the chocolate filling, taking care not to disturb the jam. Top with a second layer, jam side up, and spread with the remaining filling. Top with the final layer and press lightly.

7 Leave to set, then spread
~ the top and sides of the cake with the chocolate ganache. Decorate with chocolate curls and, if liked, chocolate-dipped physalis.

COOK'S TIP

You may find it easier to reassemble the cake in the clean cake tin. Turn it out on to a plate when set, then cover in chocolate ganache.

LACK FOREST GATEAU

This luscious light chocolate sponge, moistened with Kirsch and layered with cherries and cream, is still one of the most popular chocolate gâteaux.

INGREDIENTS

6 eggs

200g/7oz/scant 1 cup caster (superfine) sugar

5ml/1 tsp vanilla extract

50g/2oz/½ cup plain (all-purpose) flour

50g/2oz/½ cup cocoa powder

115g/4oz/½ cup unsalted butter, melted

For the filling and topping

60ml/4 tbsp Kirsch

600ml/1 pint/2½ cups double (heavy) or whipping cream

30ml/2 tbsp icing (confectioners') sugar

2.5ml/½ tsp vanilla extract

675g/1½lb jar stoned (pitted) morello cherries, drained

To decorate

icing (confectioners') sugar, for dusting

grated chocolate

chocolate curls

fresh, or drained canned, morello cherries

SERVES 8–10

1 Preheat the oven to
~ 180°C/350°F/Gas 4.
Grease three 19cm/7½in
sandwich cake tins and line
with baking parchment.
Whisk the eggs with the
sugar and vanilla in a bowl
until pale and thick, the
mixture should hold a trail
when the whisk is lifted.

2 Sift the flour and cocoa
~ over the mixture and
fold in lightly and evenly.
Stir in the melted butter.

3 Divide the mixture
~ among the cake tins and
smooth level. Bake for
15–18 minutes, until risen
and springy to the touch.
Leave to cool in the tins for
about 5 minutes, then turn
out on to wire racks and
leave to cool completely.

4 Prick each layer all over
~ with a skewer or fork,
then sprinkle over the
Kirsch. Whip the cream in
a bowl until it starts to
thicken, then beat in the
icing sugar and vanilla
extract until the mixture
begins to hold its shape.

5 To assemble, spread one
~ cake with a thick layer
of flavoured cream and a
third of cherries. Spread a
second cake with cream and
place on top of the first
layer. Add half the cherries,
then top with the final cake.

6 Spread the remaining
~ cream all over the cake.
Dust a plate with icing
sugar; position the cake.
Press grated chocolate over
the sides and decorate with
chocolate curls and cherries.

MERINGUE PYRAMID WITH CHOCOLATE MASCARPONE

INGREDIENTS

4 egg whites
pinch of salt
175g/6oz/¾ cup caster (superfine) sugar
5ml/1 tsp ground cinnamon
75g/3oz dark (bittersweet) chocolate, grated
icing (confectioners') sugar and rose petals, to decorate
For the filling
115g/4oz dark (semisweet) chocolate, broken into squares
5ml/1 tsp vanilla extract or rosewater
115g/4oz/½ cup mascarpone cheese

⌁ SERVES ABOUT 10 ⌁

Roses spell romance for this impressive cake. It makes the perfect centrepiece for a celebration buffet table, and most of the preparation can be done in advance.

1 Preheat the oven to
~ 150°C/300°F/Gas 2.
Line two large baking sheets with baking parchment. Whisk the egg whites with the salt in a clean, grease-free bowl until they form stiff peaks.

2 Gradually whisk in half
~ the sugar, then add the rest and whisk until the meringue is very stiff and glossy. Add the cinnamon and chocolate and whisk lightly to mix.

3 Draw a 20cm/8in circle
~ on the paper on one of the baking sheets, and spread the marked circle evenly with about half the meringue. Spoon the remaining meringue in 28–30 small neat heaps on both baking sheets. Bake for 1–1½ hours, or until crisp.

4 Melt the chocolate in a
~ heatproof bowl over hot water. Cool slightly, then add the vanilla extract, or rosewater, and mascarpone. Cool the mixture until it holds its shape.

5 Spoon the chocolate
~ mixture into a piping bag and sandwich the meringues together in pairs, reserving a small amount of filling for the pyramid.

6 Peel the paper from the
~ large round of meringue, then make a pile of the filled meringues on top. Keep them in position with a few dabs of the reserved filling. Dust the pyramid with icing sugar, sprinkle with the rose petals and serve at once.

COOK'S TIP

The meringues can be made up to a week in advance and stored in an airtight container in a cool, dry place.

RICH CHOCOLATE LEAF GATEAU

Thick, creamy chocolate ganache and chocolate leaves decorate this mouth-watering gâteau.

INGREDIENTS

150ml/¼ pint/⅔ cup milk
75g/3oz dark (bittersweet) chocolate, broken into squares
175g/6oz/¾ cup unsalted butter, softened
250g/9oz/1½ cups light muscovado (light brown) sugar
3 eggs
250g/9oz/2¼ cups plain (all-purpose) flour
10ml/2 tsp baking powder
75ml/5 tbsp single (light) cream
For the filling and topping
60ml/4 tbsp raspberry conserve
1 quantity Chocolate Ganache
dark and white chocolate leaves

≈ SERVES 12–14 ≈

1 Preheat the oven to
~ 190°C/375°F/Gas 5.
Grease two 22cm/8½in
sandwich cake tins and line
with baking parchment.
Melt the chocolate in the
milk over a low heat. Allow
to cool slightly.

2 Cream the butter with
~ the sugar in a bowl until
pale and fluffy. Beat in the
eggs one at a time, beating
well after each addition.

3 Sift the flour and baking
~ powder over the mixture
and fold in. Stir in the
melted chocolate mixture
and the cream.

4 Divide between the tins
~ and level the tops. Bake
for 30–35 minutes or until
the cakes are risen and firm
to the touch. Cool in the
tins for a few minutes, then
turn out on to wire racks.

COOK'S TIP

Make a mixture of dark, milk and white chocolate leaves, or marble the mixtures for a variegated effect. Prepare the chocolate leaves in advance to save time, and store them in a covered container in a cool, dry place.

5 Sandwich the cake layers
~ together with all the
raspberry conserve.

6 Spread the chocolate
~ ganache over the top
and sides of the cake. Swirl
the ganache with a knife.
Place the cake on a serving
plate, then decorate with
the dark and white
chocolate leaves.

CARIBBEAN CHOCOLATE RING WITH RUM SYRUP

INGREDIENTS

115g/4oz/½ cup unsalted butter

115g/4oz/¾ cup light muscovado (light brown) sugar

2 eggs, beaten

2 ripe bananas, mashed

30ml/2 tbsp desiccated (unsweetened shredded) coconut

30ml/2 tbsp soured cream

115g/4oz/1 cup self-rising flour

2.5ml/½ tsp bicarbonate of soda

45ml/3 tbsp cocoa

For the syrup

115g/4oz/½ cup caster (superfine) sugar

60ml/4 tbsp water

30ml/2 tbsp dark rum

50g/2oz dark (bittersweet) chocolate, chopped

To decorate

tropical fruits, such as mango, pawpaw, kiwi and physalis (Cape gooseberries)

chocolate shapes or curls

⌁ SERVES 8–10 ⌁

Lavish and colourful, this exotic chocolate gâteau can be made in advance, then, just before serving, add the syrup and fruit.

1 Preheat the oven to 180°C/350°F/Gas 4. Grease a 1.5 litre/2½ pint/ 6¼ cup ring tin.

2 Cream together the butter and sugar until light and fluffy. Beat in the eggs gradually, beating well, then mix in the bananas, coconut and cream.

3 Sift the flour, cocoa and bicarbonate of soda over the mixture and fold in thoroughly and evenly.

4 Tip into the prepared tin and spread evenly. Bake for 45–50 minutes, until firm to the touch. Cool for about 10 minutes in the tin, then turn out to finish cooling on a wire rack.

5 For the syrup, place the sugar and water in a pan and heat gently until dissolved. Bring to the boil and boil rapidly for 2 minutes. Remove from the heat.

6 Add the rum and chocolate and stir until melted and smooth, then spoon evenly over the cake.

7 Decorate the ring with tropical fruits and chocolate shapes or curls.

COOK'S TIP

For a really good chocolate flavour, use a good quality dark chocolate for the syrup.

HOCOLATE BRANDY SNAP GATEAU

INGREDIENTS

225g/8oz dark (bittersweet) chocolate, broken into squares

225g/8oz/1 cup unsalted butter, softened

200g/7oz/generous 1 cup dark muscovado (dark brown) sugar

6 eggs, separated

5ml/1 tsp vanilla extract

150g/5oz/1¼ cups ground hazelnuts

60ml/4 tbsp fresh white breadcrumbs

finely grated zest of 1 large orange

1 quantity Chocolate Ganache, for filling and frosting

icing (confectioners') sugar, for dusting

For the Brandy Snaps

50g/2oz/4 tbsp unsalted butter

50g/2oz/¼ cup caster (superfine) sugar

75g/3oz/⅓ cup golden (light corn) syrup

50g/2oz/½ cup plain (all-purpose) flour

5ml/1 tsp brandy

SERVES 8

Take your pleasure slowly by savouring every mouthful of this sensational dark chocolate gâteau topped with brandy snap frills.

1 Preheat the oven to 180°C/350°F/Gas 4. Grease two 20cm/8in sandwich cake tins and line the base of each with baking parchment. Melt the chocolate in a heatproof bowl over hot water. Remove from the heat.

2 Cream the butter with the sugar in a bowl until pale and fluffy. Beat in the egg yolks and vanilla extract. Add the chocolate and mix thoroughly.

3 In a clean, grease-free bowl, whisk the egg whites to soft peaks, then fold them into the chocolate mixture with the ground hazelnuts, the breadcrumbs and grated orange zest.

4 Divide the cake mixture between the prepared tins and smooth the tops. Bake for 25-30 minutes, or until well risen and firm. Turn out on to wire racks.

5 Make the brandy snaps. Line two baking sheets with baking parchment. Heat the butter, sugar and syrup in a saucepan over a gentle heat, stirring occasionally until smooth. Remove from the heat and stir in the flour and brandy.

6 Place small spoonfuls well apart on the baking sheets and bake for 10-15 minutes. Cool for a few seconds until firm enough to lift on to a wire rack.

7 Immediately pinch the edges of each brandy snap to make a frilled effect. If the biscuits become too firm, pop them back into the oven for a few minutes. Leave to set.

8 Sandwich the cake layers together with half the chocolate ganache, transfer to a plate and spread the remaining ganache on top.

9 Arrange the brandy snap frills over the gâteau and dust with icing sugar.

COOK'S TIP

To save time, you could use ready-made brandy snaps – simply warm them for a few minutes in the oven to make them pliable enough for shaping.

STRAWBERRY CHOCOLATE VALENTINE GATEAU

INGREDIENTS

175g/6oz/1½ cups self-rising flour

10ml/2 tsp baking powder

75ml/5 tbsp cocoa powder

115g/4oz/½ cup caster (superfine) sugar

2 eggs, beaten

15ml/1 tbsp black treacle (molasses)

150ml/¼ pint/⅔ cup sunflower oil

150ml/¼ pint/⅔ cup milk

For the filling

45ml/3 tbsp strawberry jam

150ml/¼ pint/⅔ cup double (heavy) or whipping cream

115g/4oz strawberries, sliced

To decorate

1 quantity Chocolate Fondant

chocolate hearts

icing (confectioners') sugar, for dusting

SERVES 8

Offering a slice of this voluptuous Valentine gâteau could be the start of a very special romance.

2 Add the eggs, treacle, oil and milk to the well. Mix with a spoon to combine, then beat with a hand-held electric mixer until the mixture is smooth and creamy.

3 Spoon the mixture into the prepared cake tin and spread evenly. Bake for about 45 minutes, until well risen and firm to the touch. Cool in the tin for a few minutes, then turn out on to a wire rack to cool completely.

5 Whip the cream in a bowl until it holds its shape. Stir in the strawberries, then spread over the jam. Top with the remaining cake layer.

6 Roll out the chocolate fondant and cover the cake. Decorate with chocolate hearts and dust with icing sugar.

1 Preheat the oven to 160°C/325°F/Gas 3. Grease a deep 20cm/8in heart-shaped cake tin and line the base with baking parchment. Sift the flour, baking powder and cocoa into a mixing bowl. Stir in the sugar, then make a well in the centre.

4 Using a sharp knife, slice the cake neatly into two layers. Place the bottom layer on a board or plate. Spread with strawberry jam.

COOK'S TIP

Keep the fondant covered until you are ready to use it, as the surface dries out fairly quickly, which will spoil the smooth effect.

$\mathcal{H}$OT PUDDINGS

Hot chocolate puddings appeal to anyone who craves comforting food – the sweet smell of warm chocolate from a Peachy Chocolate Bake as it cooks is hard to resist, and just the sight of proper puddings like Chocolate Chip and Banana Pudding will warm a winter's day. But if you're looking for something a little special for a dinner party, offer slices of crisp, spiced Chocolate, Date and Almond Filo Coil or luscious poached pears swathed in Chocolate Fudge Blankets.

CHOCOLATE AND ORANGE SCOTCH PANCAKES

INGREDIENTS

115g/4oz/1 cup self-rising flour
30ml/2 tbsp cocoa powder
2 eggs
50g/2oz dark (semisweet) chocolate, broken into squares
200ml/7fl oz/scant 1 cup milk
finely grated rind of 1 orange
30ml/2 tbsp orange juice
butter or oil for frying
60ml/4 tbsp chocolate curls, for sprinkling
For the sauce
2 large oranges
30ml/2 tbsp unsalted butter
45ml/3 tbsp light muscovado (light brown) sugar
250ml/8fl oz/1 cup crème fraîche
30ml/2 tbsp Grand Marnier or Cointreau
chocolate curls, to decorate

SERVES 4

Flip for these fabulous baby pancakes in a rich creamy orange liqueur sauce. Serve them straight from the pan to enjoy them at their best.

2 Mix the chocolate and
~ milk in a saucepan. Heat gently until the chocolate has melted, then beat into the batter until smooth and bubbly. Stir in the orange rind and juice.

3 Heat a large heavy-based
~ frying pan or griddle. Grease with a little butter or oil. Drop large spoonfuls of batter on to the hot surface, leaving room for spreading. Cook over a moderate heat.

4 When the pancakes are
~ lightly browned underneath and bubbly on top, flip them over to cook the other side. Slide on to a plate and keep hot, then make more in the same way.

5 Make the sauce. Grate
~ the rind of 1 orange into a bowl and set aside. Peel both oranges, taking care to remove all the pith, then slice the flesh fairly thinly.

6 Heat the butter and
~ sugar in a wide, shallow pan over a low heat, stirring until the sugar dissolves. Stir in the crème fraîche and heat gently.

7 Add the pancakes and
~ orange slices to the sauce, heat gently for 1–2 minutes, then spoon over the liqueur. Sprinkle with the reserved orange rind. Scatter over the chocolate curls and serve the pancakes at once.

1 Sift the flour and cocoa
~ into a bowl and make a well in the centre. Add the eggs and beat well, gradually incorporating the surrounding dry ingredients to make a smooth batter.

HOT CHOCOLATE ZABAGLIONE

Once you've tasted this slinky, sensuous dessert, you'll never look at cocoa in quite the same way again.

INGREDIENTS

6 egg yolks

150g/5oz/⅔ cup caster (superfine) sugar

45ml/3 tbsp cocoa powder

200ml/7fl oz/scant 1 cup Marsala

cocoa powder or icing (confectioners') sugar, for dusting

⪎ SERVES 6 ⪎

1 ~ Half fill a medium saucepan with water and bring to simmering point. Select a heatproof bowl which will fit over the pan, place the the egg yolks and sugar in it, and whisk until the mixture is pale and all the sugar has dissolved.

2 ~ Add the cocoa and Marsala, then place the bowl over the simmering water. Whisk with a hand-held electric mixer until the mixture is smooth, thick and foamy.

3 ~ Pour quickly into tall heatproof glasses, dust lightly with cocoa or icing sugar and serve immediately, with Chocolate Cinnamon Tuiles or amaretti biscuits.

RICH CHOCOLATE BRIOCHE BAKE

This scrumptious baked dessert may be based on good old bread and butter pudding, but chocolate, brioche and bitter marmalade give it superstar status.

INGREDIENTS

200g/7oz dark (semisweet) chocolate, broken into squares

60ml/4 tbsp marmalade

45ml/3 tbsp unsalted butter

4 individual brioches, or 1 large brioche loaf

3 eggs

300ml/½ pint/1¼ cups milk

300ml/½ pint/1¼ cups single (light) cream

30ml/2 tbsp demerara (raw) sugar

SERVES 4

1 Preheat the oven to ~ 180°C/350°F/Gas 4. Lightly butter a shallow ovenproof dish.

2 Melt the chocolate with ~ the marmalade and butter in a heatproof bowl over barely simmering water, stirring the mixture occasionally.

3 Slice the brioche(s), and ~ spread the melted chocolate mixture over the slices. Arrange them so that they overlap in the dish.

4 Beat the eggs, milk and ~ cream in a bowl, then pour evenly over the slices. Sprinkle with the demerara sugar and bake for 40–50 minutes, until the pudding is lightly set and bubbling. Serve hot.

COOK'S TIP

Almost any bread can be used instead of brioche, except savoury varieties. Try sliced soft white rolls, currant buns or French bread for a change.

CHOCOLATE CHIP AND BANANA PUDDING

INGREDIENTS

200g/7oz/1¾ cups self-rising flour

75g/3oz/6 tbsp unsalted butter

2 ripe bananas

75g/3oz/⅓ cup caster (superfine) sugar

60ml/4 tbsp milk

1 egg, beaten

60ml/4 tbsp dark (semisweet) chocolate chips or chopped chocolate

Glossy Chocolate Sauce, to serve

~ SERVES 4 ~

Hot and steamy, this superb light pudding has a beguiling banana and chocolate flavour.

1 Prepare a steamer or half ~ fill a saucepan with water and bring it to the boil. Grease a 1 litre/1¾ pint/4 cup pudding basin. Sift the flour into a bowl and rub in the unsalted butter with your fingertips, until the mixture resembles coarse breadcrumbs.

2 Mash the bananas in a ~ bowl. Stir them into the creamed mixture, with the caster sugar.

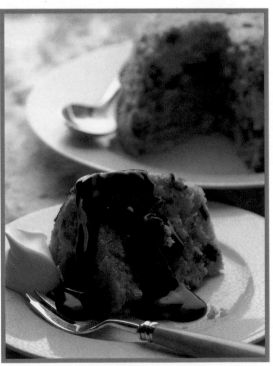

3 Whisk the milk with the ~ egg in a jug or bowl, then beat into the pudding mixture. Stir in the chocolate chips or pieces.

4 Spoon the mixture into ~ the prepared basin, cover closely with a double thickness of foil, and steam for 2 hours, topping up the water as required during cooking.

5 Run a knife around the ~ top of the pudding to loosen it, then turn it out on to a serving dish. Serve hot, with chocolate sauce.

COOK'S TIP

If you have a food processor, make a quick-mix version by processing all the ingredients, except the chocolate, until smooth. Stir in the chocolate and proceed as in the recipe.

M AGIC CHOCOLATE MUD PUDDING

INGREDIENTS

50g/2oz/4 tbsp butter

200g/7oz/generous 1 cup light
muscovado (light brown) sugar

475ml/16fl oz/2 cups milk

90g/3½oz/scant 1 cup self-rising flour

5ml/1 tsp ground cinnamon

75ml/5 tbsp cocoa powder

Greek-style (US strained, plain) yogurt
or vanilla ice cream, to serve

☞ SERVES 4 ☜

*A popular favourite, which magically
separates into a light and luscious sponge
and a velvety chocolate sauce.*

1 Preheat the oven to
~ 180°C/350°F/Gas 4.
Lightly grease a 1.5 litre/
2½ pint/6 cup ovenproof
dish and place on a baking
sheet.

2 Place the butter in a
~ saucepan. Add 115g/
4oz/¾ cup of the sugar and
150ml/¼ pint/⅔ cup of the
milk. Heat gently, stirring
from time to time, until the
butter has melted and all the
sugar has dissolved. Remove
the pan from the heat.

3 Sift the flour, cinnamon
~ and 15 ml/1 tbsp of the
cocoa powder into the pan
and stir into the mixture,
mixing evenly. Pour the
mixture into the prepared
dish and level the surface.

4 Sift the remaining sugar
~ and cocoa into a bowl,
mix well, then sprinkle over
the pudding mixture.

5 Pour the remaining milk
~ over the pudding.

6 Bake for 45–50 minutes
~ or until the sponge has
risen and is firm to the
touch. Serve hot, with the
yogurt or ice cream.

COOK'S TIP

*A soufflé dish or similar
straight-sided ovenproof
dish is ideal for this, since
it supports the sponge as
it rises above the sauce.*

CHOCOLATE CREPES WITH PLUMS AND PORT

INGREDIENTS

50g/2oz dark (semisweet) chocolate, broken into squares

200ml/7fl oz/scant 1 cup milk

120ml/4fl oz/½ cup single (light) cream

30ml/2 tbsp cocoa powder

115g/4oz/1 cup plain (all-purpose) flour

2 eggs

For the filling

500g/1¼ lb red or golden plums

50g/2oz/¼ cup caster (superfine) sugar

30ml/2 tbsp water

30ml/2 tbsp port

oil, for frying

175g/6oz/¾ cup crème fraîche

For the sauce

150g/5oz dark (semisweet) chocolate, broken into squares

175ml/6fl oz/¾ cup double (heavy) cream

SERVES 6

A good dinner party dessert, this dish can be made in advance and always looks impressive.

1 Heat the chocolate in a saucepan, with the milk, until melted. Pour into a blender or food processor and add the cream, cocoa powder, flour and eggs. Process, then tip into a jug and chill for 30 minutes.

2 Halve and stone the plums. Place them in a saucepan and add the sugar and water. Bring to the boil, then lower the heat, cover, and simmer for about 10 minutes or until the plums are tender. Stir in the port; simmer for a further 30 seconds. Remove from the heat and keep warm.

COOK'S TIP

Vary the fruit according to what is in season, using a complementary liqueur or spirit. Try cherries with cherry brandy, mandarin orange segments with Grand Marnier or poached pears or apples with Calvados. All will taste wonderful with chocolate.

3 Have ready a sheet baking parchment. Heat a crêpe pan, grease it lightly with a little oil, then pour in just enough batter to cover the base of the pan, swirling to coat evenly. Cook until the crêpe has set, then flip it over to cook the other side. Slide the crêpe out on to the sheet of paper, then cook 9–11 more crêpes in the same way.

4 To make the sauce, mix the chocolate and cream in a saucepan. Heat gently, stirring until smooth. Add the port and heat gently, stirring, for 1 minute.

5 Divide the plum filling between the crêpes, add a dollop of crème fraîche to each and roll them up carefully. Serve in individual bowls, with the chocolate sauce spooned over the top.

CHOCOLATE ALMOND MERINGUE PIE

INGREDIENTS

175g/6oz/1½ cups plain (all-purpose) flour

50g/2oz/⅓ cup ground rice (rice flour)

150g/5oz/⅔ cup unsalted butter

finely grated zest of 1 orange

1 egg yolk

flaked almonds and melted dark (bittersweet) chocolate, to decorate

For the filling

150g/5oz dark (bittersweet) chocolate, broken into squares

50g/2oz/4 tbsp unsalted butter, softened

75g/3oz/⅓ cup caster (superfine) sugar

10ml/2 tsp cornflour (cornstarch)

4 egg yolks

75g/3oz/¾ cup ground almonds

For the meringue

3 egg whites

150g/5oz/⅔ cup caster (superfine) sugar

SERVES 6

Treat your tastebuds to the contrasting textures and flavours of fluffy meringue on a velvety smooth chocolate filling in a light orange pastry crust.

1 Sift the flour and ground
~ rice into a bowl. Rub in the butter until it resembles breadcrumbs. Add the orange zest and egg yolk to bring the dough together. Roll out and line a 23cm/9in round flan tin. Chill.

2 Preheat the oven to
~ 190°C/375°F/Gas 5. Prick the pastry base with a fork, cover with baking parchment weighed down with baking beans and bake for 10 minutes. Remove the pastry case; take out the baking beans and paper.

3 Melt the chocolate in a
~ heatproof bowl over hot water. Cream the butter with the sugar in a bowl, then beat in the cornflour and egg yolks. Fold in the almonds, then chocolate. Spread in the pastry case. Bake for 10 minutes.

4 Make the meringue.
~ Whisk the egg whites in a clean, bowl until stiff, then gradually whisk in about half the caster sugar. Fold in the remaining sugar.

5 Spoon the meringue
~ over the chocolate filling, lifting with the back of the spoon to form peaks. Reduce the oven to 180°C/350°F/Gas 4 and bake the pie for 15-20 minutes or until the topping is pale gold. Serve warm, scattered with almonds and drizzled with melted chocolate.

COOK'S TIP

The pastry can be made in a food processor. Pulse all the ingredients in the processor for a few seconds until the pastry just binds together. If too dry, add 5–10ml/1–2 tsp water.

CHOCOLATE, DATE AND ALMOND FILO COIL

275g/10oz packet filo pastry, thawed if frozen

50g/2oz/4 tbsp unsalted butter, melted

icing sugar, cocoa powder and ground cinnamon, for dusting

For the filling

75g/3oz/6 tbsp unsalted butter

115g/4oz dark (bittersweet) chocolate, broken into squares

115g/4oz/1 cup ground almonds

115g/4oz/⅔ cup chopped dates

75g/3oz/⅔ cup icing (confectioners') sugar

10ml/2 tsp rosewater

2.5ml/½ tsp ground cinnamon

SERVES 6

Experience the allure of the Middle East with this delectable dessert. Crisp filo pastry conceals a chocolate and rosewater filling studded with dates and almonds.

1 Preheat the oven to
~ 180°C/350°F/Gas 4.
Grease a 22cm/8½in round cake tin. Make the filling. Melt the butter with the chocolate in a heatproof bowl over barely simmering water, then remove from the heat and stir in the remaining ingredients to make a thick paste. Leave to cool.

2 Lay one sheet of filo on
~ a clean work surface (see Cook's Tip). Brush it with melted butter, then lay a second sheet on top and brush with butter.

3 Roll a handful of the
~ chocolate almond mixture into a long sausage shape and place along one long edge of the layered filo. Roll the pastry up tightly to make a roll.

4 Place the roll around the
~ outside of the tin. Make enough rolls to fill the tin.

5 Brush the coil with the
~ remaining melted butter. Bake for 30–35 minutes until the pastry is golden brown and crisp. Remove the coil from the tin; place it on a plate. Serve warm, dusted with icing sugar, cocoa and cinnamon.

COOK'S TIP

Filo pastry dries out very quickly, so remove one sheet at a time and keep the rest covered with a slightly damp, clean dish towel.

$\mathcal{P}$EARS IN CHOCOLATE FUDGE BLANKETS

INGREDIENTS

6 ripe pears
30ml/2 tbsp lemon juice
75g/3oz/⅓ cup caster (superfine) sugar
300ml/½ pint/1¼ cups water
1 cinnamon stick
For the sauce
200ml/7fl oz/scant 1 cup double (heavy) cream
150g/5oz/scant 1 cup light muscovado (light brown) sugar
25g/1oz/2 tbsp unsalted butter
60ml/4 tbsp golden (light corn) syrup
120ml/4fl oz/½ cup milk
200g/7oz dark (bittersweet) chocolate, broken into squares

✿ SERVES 6 ✿

1 Peel the pears. Scoop
~ out the cores from the base. Brush with lemon juice to prevent browning.

2 Heat the sugar and water
~ in a large saucepan until the sugar dissolves. Add the pears and cinnamon stick with any remaining lemon juice, and, if necessary, a little more water, so that the pears are almost covered.

3 Bring to the boil, then
~ lower the heat, cover the pan and simmer the pears gently for 15-20 minutes, or until they are just tender.

4 Meanwhile, make the
~ sauce. Place the cream, sugar, butter, syrup and milk in a heavy saucepan. Heat gently until the sugar has dissolved and the butter and syrup have melted, then bring to the boil.

5 Boil, stirring constantly,
~ for about 5 minutes or until the sauce is thick and smooth. Remove from the heat and stir in the chocolate, a few squares at a time, until melted.

6 Using a slotted spoon,
~ transfer the poached pears to a dish. Keep hot. Boil the syrup rapidly to reduce to about 45-60ml/ 3-4 tbsp. Remove the cinnamon stick and stir the syrup into the sauce.

7 Serve the pears in
~ individual bowls, with the hot chocolate fudge sauce spooned over.

PEACHY CHOCOLATE BAKE

Resist everything except temptation, Oscar Wilde urged. So next time you crave something hot and chocolatey, raid the storecupboard and whip up this delicious pudding.

INGREDIENTS

200g/7oz dark (bittersweet) chocolate, broken into squares

115g/4oz/½ cup unsalted butter

4 eggs, separated

115g/4oz/½ cup caster (superfine) sugar

425g/15oz can peach slices, drained

SERVES 6

1 Preheat the oven to 160°C/325°F/Gas 3. Butter a wide ovenproof dish. Melt the chocolate with the butter in a heatproof bowl over barely simmering water. Remove from the heat.

2 In a bowl, whisk the egg yolks with the sugar until thick and pale. In a clean, grease-free bowl, whisk the whites until stiff.

3 Beat the chocolate into the egg yolk mixture.

4 Fold in the whites lightly and evenly.

5 Fold the peach slices into the mixture, then tip into the prepared dish.

6 Bake for 35-40 minutes, or until risen and just firm. Serve hot, with cream or yogurt if liked.

COOK'S TIP

Don't level the mixture in the dish before baking, as it looks more interesting if the surface is rough and uneven.

𝒫 RUNE BEIGNETS IN CHOCOLATE ARMAGNAC SAUCE

INGREDIENTS

75g/3oz/¾ cup plain (all-purpose) flour
45ml/3 tbsp ground almonds
45ml/3 tbsp oil or melted butter
1 egg white
60ml/4 tbsp water
oil for deep frying
175g/6oz/¾ cup ready-to-eat stoned prunes
45ml/3 tbsp vanilla sugar
15ml/1 tbsp cocoa powder
For the sauce
200g/7oz milk chocolate, broken into squares
120ml/4fl oz/½ cup crème fraîche
30ml/2 tbsp Armagnac or brandy

SERVES 4

COOK'S TIP

Vanilla sugar is very popular in parts of Europe, where it is sold in sachets. To make your own, add a vanilla pod to a jar of caster sugar. The sugar will soon take on a subtle vanilla flavour.

Go on, indulge yourself! Slide your spoon into silky chocolate sauce, scoop up a feather-light prune beignet and get ready for rapture.

1 First make the sauce.
~ Melt the chocolate in a heatproof bowl over hot water. Remove from the heat, stir in the crème fraîche, then add the Armagnac. Replace the bowl over the water (off the heat) so that it stays warm.

2 Beat the flour, almonds,
~ oil or butter and egg white in a bowl, then beat in enough of the water to make a smooth, thick batter.

3 Heat the oil for deep
~ frying to 180°C/350°F or until a cube of dried bread browns in 30-45 seconds. Coat the prunes in batter and fry, a few at a time, until the beignets rise to the surface of the oil and are golden brown and crisp.

4 Remove each successive
~ batch of beignets with a slotted spoon, drain on kitchen paper and keep hot. Mix the vanilla sugar and cocoa in a bowl or stout paper bag, add the drained beignets and toss well to coat.

5 Serve in individual
~ bowls, with the sauce poured over the top.

HOT MOCHA RUM SOUFFLES

INGREDIENTS

25g/1oz/2 tbsp unsalted butter, melted

65g/2½oz/generous ½ cup cocoa powder

75g/3oz/⅓ cup caster (superfine) sugar

60ml/4 tbsp strong black coffee

30ml/2 tbsp dark rum

6 egg whites

icing (confectioners') sugar, for dusting

⌒ SERVES 6 ⌒

These superb soufflés always rise to the occasion. Serve them as soon as they are cooked for a fantastic finale to a dinner party.

1 Preheat the oven and a
~ baking tray to 190°C/
375°F/Gas 5. Grease six
250ml/8fl oz/1 cup soufflé
dishes with melted butter.

2 Mix 15ml/1 tbsp of the
~ cocoa with 15ml/1 tbsp
of the caster sugar in a
bowl. Tip the mixture into
each of the dishes in turn,
rotating them so that they
are evenly
coated.

3 Mix the remaining cocoa
~ with the coffee and rum.

4 Whisk the egg whites in
~ a clean, grease-free bowl
until they form peaks.
Whisk in the remaining
caster sugar. Stir a spoonful
of the whites into the cocoa
mixture to lighten it, then
fold in the remaining whites.

5 Spoon the mixture into
~ the prepared dishes,
smoothing the tops. Place
on the hot baking tray, and
bake for 12–15 minutes or
until risen. Serve at once,
dusted with icing sugar.

COOK'S TIP

*When serving the soufflés
at the end of a dinner
party, prepare them just
before the meal is served.
Pop in the oven as soon
as the main course is
finished and serve
freshly baked.*

STEAMED CHOCOLATE AND FRUIT PUDDINGS WITH CHOCOLATE SYRUP

Some things always turn out well, including these wonderful little puddings. Dark, fluffy chocolate sponge is topped with tangy cranberries and apple, and served with a honeyed chocolate syrup.

INGREDIENTS

115g/4oz/⅔ cup dark muscovado (dark brown) sugar

1 eating apple

75g/3oz/¾ cup cranberries, thawed if frozen

115g/4oz/½ cup butter, softened

2 eggs

75g/3oz/¾ cup plain (all-purpose) flour

2.5ml/½ tsp baking powder

45ml/3 tbsp cocoa powder

For the Chocolate Syrup

115g/4oz dark (bittersweet) chocolate, broken into squares

30ml/2 tbsp clear honey

15ml/1 tbsp unsalted butter

2.5ml/½ tsp vanilla extract

☞ SERVES 4 ☜

1 Prepare a steamer or half fill a saucepan with water and bring it to the boil. Grease four individual pudding basins and sprinkle each one with a little of the muscovado sugar to coat well all over.

2 Peel and core the apple. Dice it into a bowl, add the cranberries and mix well. Divide among the prepared pudding basins.

3 Place the remaining muscovado sugar in a mixing bowl. Add the butter, eggs, flour, baking powder and cocoa; beat until combined and smooth.

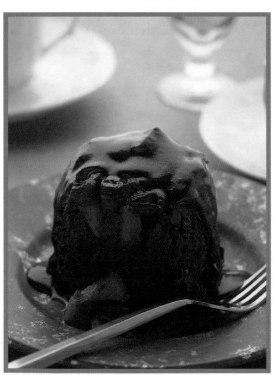

4 Spoon the mixture into the basins and cover each with a double thickness of foil. Steam for about 45 minutes, topping up the boiling water as required, until the puddings are well risen and firm.

5 Make the syrup. Mix the chocolate, honey, butter and vanilla in a small pan. Heat gently, stirring, until melted and smooth.

6 Run a knife around the edge of each pudding to loosen, then turn out on to individual plates. Serve with the chocolate syrup.

COOK'S TIP

The puddings can be quickly cooked in the microwave. Use non-metallic basins and cover with greaseproof paper instead of foil. Cook on High (100% power) for 5–6 minutes, then allow to stand for 2-3 minutes before turning out.

COLD DESSERTS

Cold desserts mean easy entertaining as they can mostly be prepared ahead. A rich, dark Chocolate Sorbet with Red Fruits can be made days in advance, ready to scoop and serve with fresh red fruits, or a Black and White Chocolate Mousse will keep in the fridge for the next day. But don't stop at mousses and ices – if your sweet tooth craves a really lavish treat, how about Raspberry, Mascarpone and White Chocolate Cheesecake, or, for more formal meals, an elegant Chocolate Hazelnut Galette?

CHOCOLATE SORBET WITH RED FRUITS

The chill that thrills — that's chocolate sorbet. For a really fine texture, it helps to have an ice-cream maker, which churns the mixture as it freezes, but you can make it by hand quite easily.

INGREDIENTS

475ml/16fl oz/2 cups water

45ml/3 tbsp clear honey

115g/4oz/½ cup caster (superfine) sugar

75g/3oz/¾ cup cocoa powder

50g/2oz dark (bittersweet) chocolate, broken into squares

400g/14oz soft red fruits, such as raspberries, redcurrants or strawberries

⌘ SERVES 6 ⌘

1 Place the water, honey, sugar and cocoa in a saucepan. Heat gently, stirring occasionally, until the sugar has completely dissolved.

2 Remove the pan from the heat, add the chocolate and stir until melted. Leave until cool.

COOK'S TIP

This sorbet looks attractive if served in small oval scoops shaped with two spoons — simply scoop out the sorbet with one tablespoon, then use another to smooth it off and transfer it to the plate.

3 Tip into an ice-cream maker and churn until frozen. Alternatively, pour into a container suitable for use in the freezer, freeze until slushy, whisk until smooth, then freeze again. Whisk for a second time before the mixture hardens completely. Transfer to a plastic container.

4 Remove the sorbet from the freezer 10–15 minutes before serving, so that it softens slightly. Serve the sorbet in scoops, with the soft fruits.

R ASPBERRY, MASCARPONE AND WHITE CHOCOLATE CHEESECAKE

INGREDIENTS

50g/2oz/4 tbsp unsalted butter

225g/8oz ginger nut cookies, crushed

50g/2oz/½ cup chopped pecan nuts or walnuts

For the filling

275g/10oz/1¼ cups mascarpone cheese

175g/6oz/¾ cup ricotta cheese

2 eggs, beaten

45ml/3 tbsp caster (superfine) sugar

250g/9oz white chocolate, broken into squares

225g/8oz/1½ cups fresh or frozen raspberries

For the topping

115g/4oz/½ cup mascarpone cheese

75g/3oz/⅓ cup ricotta cheese

white chocolate curls and raspberries, to decorate

SERVES 8

Raspberries and white chocolate are an irresistible combination, especially when teamed with rich mascarpone on a crunchy ginger and pecan nut base.

1 Preheat the oven to 150°C/300°F/Gas 2. Melt the butter in a pan, then stir in the crushed cookies and nuts. Press into the base of a 23cm/9in springform cake tin.

2 Make the filling. Beat the mascarpone and ricotta cheese in a bowl, then beat in the eggs and caster sugar until combined.

3 Melt the white chocolate gently in a heatproof bowl over hot water, then stir into the cheese mixture with the fresh or frozen raspberries.

4 Tip into the prepared tin and spread evenly, then bake for about 1 hour or until just set. Switch off the oven, but do not remove the cheesecake. Leave it until cold and set.

5 Remove the sides of the tin and carefully lift the cheesecake on to a plate. Make the topping by mixing the mascarpone and ricotta cheese in a bowl and then spreading over the top of the cheesecake. Finally, decorate with chocolate curls and raspberries.

COOK'S TIP

The biscuits for the base should be crushed quite finely. This can easily be done in a food processor. Alternatively place the biscuits in a stout plastic bag and crush them with a rolling pin.

DEVILISH CHOCOLATE ROULADE

A decadent dessert for a party or a dinner à deux: the roulade can be made a day or two ahead, then filled and rolled on the day of serving.

INGREDIENTS

175g/6oz dark (bittersweet) chocolate, broken into squares

4 eggs, separated

115g/4oz/½ cup caster (superfine) sugar

cocoa powder for dusting

For the filling

225g/8oz dark (semisweet) chocolate, broken into squares

45ml/3 tbsp brandy

2 eggs, separated

250g/9oz/generous 1 cup mascarpone cheese

chocolate-dipped strawberries, to decorate

~ SERVES 6–8 ~

1 Preheat the oven to 180°C/350°F/Gas 4. Grease a 33 x 23cm/13 x 9in Swiss roll tin and line with baking parchment. Melt the chocolate in a heatproof bowl.

2 Whisk the egg yolks and sugar in a bowl until pale and thick, then stir in the melted chocolate evenly.

3 In a clean, grease-free bowl, whisk the egg whites to soft peaks, then fold evenly into the egg and chocolate mixture.

4 Scrape into the tin and spread evenly. Bake for 15-20 minutes, until risen and firm to the touch. Dust a sheet of baking parchment with cocoa. Turn the sponge out on the paper, cover with a clean dish towel and leave to cool.

COOK'S TIP

Don't worry if the roulade cracks – it's meant to!

5 Make the filling. Melt the chocolate with the brandy in a heatproof bowl over hot water. Remove from the heat. Beat the egg yolks together, then beat into the chocolate mixture. In a separate bowl, whisk the whites to soft peaks, then fold them lightly and evenly into the filling.

6 Uncover the roulade, remove the lining paper and spread with the mascarpone. Spread the chocolate mixture over the top, then roll up carefully from a long side to enclose the filling. Transfer to a serving plate, top with fresh chocolate-dipped strawberries and dust with cocoa powder.

TIRAMISU IN CHOCOLATE CUPS

INGREDIENTS

1 egg yolk

30ml/2 tbsp caster (superfine) sugar

2.5ml/½ tsp vanilla extract

250g/9oz/generous 1 cup
mascarpone cheese

120ml/4fl oz/½ cup strong black coffee

15ml/1 tbsp cocoa powder

30ml/2 tbsp coffee liqueur

16 amaretti cookies

cocoa powder, for dusting

For the Chocolate Cups

175g/6oz dark (bittersweet) chocolate,
broken into squares

25g/1oz/2 tbsp unsalted butter

SERVES 6

1 Make the chocolate
~ cups. Cut out six
15cm/6in rounds of baking
parchment. Melt the
chocolate with the butter in
a heatproof bowl, over
barely simmering water.
Stir until smooth, then
spread a spoonful of the
chocolate mixture over each
circle, to within 2cm/¾in of
the edge.

*Give in to the temptation of tiramisu,
with its magical mocha flavour.*

2 Carefully lift each paper
~ round and drape it over
an upturned teacup or
ramekin so that the edges
curve into frills. Leave until
completely set, then
carefully lift off and peel
away the paper to reveal the
chocolate cups.

3 Make the filling. Beat
~ the egg yolk and sugar
in a bowl until smooth,
then stir in the vanilla
extract and mascarpone.
Mix to a smooth creamy
consistency.

4 In a separate bowl, mix
~ the coffee, cocoa and
liqueur. Break up the
amaretti roughly, then stir
into the mixture.

5 Place the chocolate cups
~ on plates. Divide half
the amaretti mixture among
them, then spoon over half
the mascarpone mixture.
Spoon over the remaining
amaretti mixture (with any
liquid), top with the rest of
the mascarpone mixture and
dust with cocoa. Serve as
soon as possible.

COOK'S TIP

*When spreading the
chocolate for the cups,
don't aim for perfectly
regular edges; uneven
edges will give a more
frilled effect.*

CHOCOLATE ORANGE MARQUISE

INGREDIENTS

200g/7oz/scant 1 cup caster (superfine) sugar

60ml/4 tbsp freshly squeezed orange juice

350g/12oz dark (bittersweet) chocolate, broken into squares

225g/8oz/1 cup unsalted butter, cubed

5 eggs

finely grated zest of 1 orange

45ml/3 tbsp plain (all-purpose) flour

icing sugar and finely pared strips of orange rind, to decorate

SERVES 6–8

1 Preheat the oven to 180°C/350°F/Gas 4. Grease a 23cm/9in round cake tin with a depth of 6cm/2½in. Line the base with baking parchment.

2 Place 115g/4oz/½ cup of the sugar in a saucepan. Add the orange juice and stir over a gentle heat until the sugar has dissolved.

3 Remove from the heat and stir in the chocolate until melted, then add the butter, cube by cube, until thoroughly melted and evenly mixed.

COOK'S TIP

The safest way to add the water to the roasting tin is to place the tin on a shelf in the oven, pull the shelf out slightly, then pour in freshly boiled water from a kettle. If you pour the water in before moving it to the oven, there is a risk of spills and scalds.

4 Whisk the eggs with the remaining sugar in a large bowl until pale and very thick. Add the orange zest. Then, using a metal spoon, fold the chocolate mixture lightly and evenly into the egg mixture. Sift the flour over the top and fold in evenly.

5 Scrape the mixture into the prepared tin. Place in a roasting pan, transfer to the oven, then pour hot water into the roasting pan to reach about halfway up the sides of the cake tin, to create a bain marie.

6 Bake for about 1 hour or until the cake is firm to the touch. Remove the cake tin from the bain marie and cool for 15-20 minutes. To turn out, invert the cake on a baking sheet, place a serving plate upside down on top, then turn plate and baking sheet over together so that the cake is transferred to the plate.

7 Dust with icing sugar, decorate with strips of pared orange rind and serve slightly warm or cold.

ROCKY ROAD ICE CREAM

For chills and thrills, there's nothing to beat this classic sweet ice cream packed with contrasting textures and flavours.

INGREDIENTS

115g/4oz dark (semisweet) chocolate, broken into squares

150ml/¼ pint/⅔ cup milk

300ml/½ pint/1¼ cups double (heavy) cream

115g/4oz/1½ cups marshmallows, chopped

50g/2oz/½ cup glacé (candied) cherries, chopped

50g/2oz/½ cup crumbled shortbread

30ml/2 tbsp chopped walnuts

⮞ SERVES 6 ⮜

2 Whip the cream in a bowl until it just holds its shape. Beat in the chocolate mixture.

4 Stir the marshmallows, cherries, crumbled shortbread and nuts into the iced mixture, then return to the freezer container and freeze until firm.

5 Allow the ice cream to soften at room temperature for 15-20 minutes before serving in scoops.

1 Melt the chocolate in the milk in a saucepan over a gentle heat, stirring from time to time. Leave to cool completely.

3 Tip the mixture into an ice cream maker and churn until thick and almost frozen. Alternatively, pour into a container suitable for use in the freezer, freeze until ice crystals form around the edges, then whisk until smooth.

> **COOK'S TIP**
>
> *For a quick version, simply stir the flavourings into bought soft-scoop chocolate ice cream and freeze until firm.*

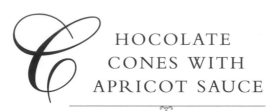

CHOCOLATE CONES WITH APRICOT SAUCE

INGREDIENTS

250g/9oz dark (bittersweet) chocolate, broken into squares

350g/12oz/1½ cups ricotta cheese

45ml/3 tbsp double (heavy) cream

30ml/2 tbsp brandy

30ml/2 tbsp icing (confectioners') sugar

finely grated rind of 1 lemon

strips of lemon zest, to decorate

For the sauce

175g/6oz/⅔ cup apricot jam

45ml/3 tbsp lemon juice

⌐ SERVES 6 ⌐

The seductive liaison of dark chocolate wrapped around a creamy brandy-flavoured filling makes a dramatic and delicious dessert. The cones can be made, filled and arranged with the sauce on plates before you start your meal, then chilled ready to serve.

1 Cut 12 x 10cm/4in
~ double thickness rounds from baking parchment and shape each into a cone. Secure with masking tape.

2 Melt the chocolate in a
~ heatproof bowl over hot water, cool slightly, then spoon a little into each cone, swirling and brushing it to coat the paper in an even layer.

3 Stand each cone point
~ downwards in a glass, to hold it straight. Leave in a cool place until the cones are completely set.

4 For the sauce, combine
~ the apricot jam and lemon juice in a small pan. Melt gently, then cool.

5 Beat the ricotta, cream,
~ brandy and icing sugar in a bowl. Add the lemon zest.

6 Spoon or pipe the
~ ricotta mixture into the cones, then carefully peel off the baking parchment.

7 Serve the cones in pairs
~ on individual plates, scattered with lemon rind and surrounded with the cooled apricot sauce.

COOK'S TIP

When making the paper cones, make sure there is no gap at the pointed end or the chocolate will run out when you coat them. It is best to let the chocolate cool slightly before use, so that it sets quickly.

WHITE CHOCOLATE VANILLA MOUSSE WITH DARK CHOCOLATE SAUCE

Happy endings are assured when slices of creamy white chocolate mousse are served with a divine dark sauce.

INGREDIENTS

200g/7oz white chocolate, broken into squares

2 eggs, separated

60ml/4 tbsp caster (superfine) sugar

300ml/½ pint/1¼ cups double (heavy) cream

1 packet powdered gelatine

150ml/5fl oz/⅔ cup Greek-style (US strained, plain) yogurt

10ml/2 tsp vanilla extract

For the sauce

50g/2oz dark (semisweet) chocolate, broken into squares

30ml/2 tbsp dark rum

60ml/4 tbsp single (light) cream

⌐ SERVES 6 – 8 ⌐

COOK'S TIP

It is very important to make sure that the gelatine is completely dissolved in the cream before adding to the other ingredients. Lift a little of the mixture on a wooden spoon to check that no undissolved granules remain. Alternatively, soften the gelatine in 30ml/2 tbsp cold water in a cup, then melt it over hot water before stirring it into the heated cream.

1 Line a 1 litre/1¾ pint/ 4 cup loaf tin with non-stick baking paper or clear film. Melt the chocolate in a heatproof bowl over hot water, then remove from the heat.

2 Whisk the egg yolks and sugar in a bowl until pale and thick, then beat in the melted chocolate.

3 Heat the cream in a small saucepan until almost boiling, then remove from the heat. Sprinkle the powdered gelatine over, stirring until completely dissolved.

4 Then pour on to the chocolate mixture, whisking vigorously to mix until smooth.

5 Whisk the yogurt and vanilla extract into the mixture. In a clean, grease-free bowl, whisk the egg whites until stiff, then fold them into the mixture. Tip into the prepared loaf tin, level the surface and chill until set.

6 Make the sauce. Melt the chocolate with the rum and cream in a heatproof bowl over barely simmering water, stirring occasionally, then leave to cool completely.

7 When the mousse is set, remove it from the tin with the aid of the paper or clear film. Serve in thick slices with the cooled chocolate sauce.

I TALIAN CHOCOLATE RICOTTA PIE

INGREDIENTS

225g/8oz/2 cups plain (all-purpose) flour

30ml/2 tbsp cocoa powder

60ml/4 tbsp caster (superfine) sugar

115g/4oz/½ cup unsalted butter

60ml/4 tbsp dry sherry

For the filling

2 egg yolks

115g/4oz/½ cup caster (superfine) sugar

500g/1¼lb/2½ cups ricotta cheese

finely grated zest of 1 lemon

90ml/6 tbsp dark chocolate chips

75ml/5 tbsp chopped candied peel

45ml/3 tbsp chopped angelica

SERVES 6

1 Preheat the oven to ~ 200°C/400°F/Gas 6. Sift the flour and cocoa into a bowl and add the sugar. Rub in the butter until the mixture resembles crumbs, then work in the sherry to bind to a firm dough.

2 Roll out three-quarters ~ of the pastry on a lightly floured surface and line a 24cm/9½in loose-based flan tin.

3 Make the filling. Beat ~ the egg yolks and sugar in a bowl, then beat in the ricotta to mix thoroughly. Stir in the lemon zest, chocolate chips, candied peel and angelica.

4 Scrape the ricotta ~ mixture into the pastry case and level the surface. Roll out the remaining pastry and cut into strips, then arrange these in a lattice over the pie.

5 Bake for 15 minutes, ~ then lower the oven temperature to 180°C/ 350°F/Gas 4 and cook for a further 30-35 minutes, until golden brown and firm. Cool in the tin.

*C*OOK'S *T*IP

This pie is best served at room temperature, so if you make it in advance, chill it when cool, then bring to room temperature for about 30 minutes before serving.

CHOCOLATE MANDARIN TRIFLE

INGREDIENTS

4 trifle sponges (ladyfingers)

14 amaretti

60ml/4 tbsp Amaretto di Saronno
or sweet sherry

8 mandarin oranges

For the custard

200g/7oz dark (semisweet) chocolate,
broken into squares

30ml/2 tbsp cornflour (cornstarch) or
custard powder

30ml/2 tbsp caster (superfine) sugar

2 egg yolks

200ml/7fl oz/scant 1 cup milk

250g/9oz/generous 1 cup
mascarpone cheese

For the topping

250g/9oz/generous 1 cup ricotta
cheese

chocolate shapes

mandarin segments

SERVES 6–8

Trifle is always a tempting treat, but when a rich chocolate and mascarpone custard is combined with amaretto and mandarin oranges, it becomes sheer delight.

2 Squeeze the juice from 2 mandarins and sprinkle into the dish. Peel and segment the rest and put in the dish.

1 Break up the trifle sponges and place them in a large glass serving dish. Crumble the amaretti over and then sprinkle with amaretto or sweet sherry.

3 Make the custard. Melt the chocolate in a heatproof bowl over hot water. In a separate bowl, mix the cornflour or custard powder, sugar and egg yolks to a paste.

4 Heat the milk in a small saucepan until almost boiling, then pour on to the egg yolk mixture, stirring constantly. Return to the clean pan and stir over a low heat until the custard has thickened slightly and is smooth.

5 Stir in the mascarpone until melted, then add the melted chocolate, mixing it evenly. Spread evenly over the trifle, cool, then chill until set.

6 To finish, spread the ricotta cheese over the custard. Decorate with chocolate shapes and mandarin segments just before serving.

CHOCOLATE AND CHESTNUT POTS

INGREDIENTS

250g/9oz dark (semisweet) chocolate

60ml/4 tbsp Madeira

25g/1oz/2 tbsp butter, diced

2 eggs, separated

225g/8oz/1 cup unsweetened chestnut purée

crème fraîche or whipped double (heavy) cream, to decorate

~ SERVES 6 ~

These rich little pots, prepared in advance, are the perfect ending for a dinner party. For the very best flavour, remove them from the fridge about 30 minutes before serving, to allow them to "ripen".

1 Make a few chocolate
~ curls for decoration, then break the rest of the chocolate into squares and melt it with the Madeira in a saucepan over a gentle heat. Remove from the heat and add the butter, a few pieces at a time, stirring until melted and smooth.

COOK'S TIP

If Madeira is not available, use brandy or rum. The chocolate pots can be frozen successfully for up to 2 months.

2 Beat the egg yolks
~ quickly into the mixture, then beat in the chestnut purée, mixing until smooth.

3 Whisk the egg whites in
~ a clean, grease-free bowl until stiff. Stir about 15ml/ 1 tbsp of the whites into the chestnut mixture to lighten it, then fold in the rest evenly.

4 Spoon the mixture into
~ six small ramekin dishes and chill until set. Serve the pots topped with a generous spoonful of crème fraîche or whipped double cream. Decorate with the dark chocolate curls.

CHOCOLATE, BANANA AND TOFFEE PIE

Chocoholics love finding new ways of using their favourite ingredient. Here's how it can help to make the famous Banoffee Pie even more delicious.

INGREDIENTS

65g/2½oz/5 tbsp unsalted butter

250g/9oz milk chocolate digestive biscuits (wafer cookies)

chocolate curls, to decorate

For the filling

397g/13oz can condensed milk

150g/5oz dark (semisweet) chocolate, broken into squares

120ml/4fl oz/½ cup crème fraîche or single (light) cream

15ml/1 tbsp golden (light corn) syrup

For the topping

2 bananas

250ml/8fl oz/1 cup crème fraîche

10ml/2 tbsp strong black coffee

~ SERVES 6 ~

1 Melt the unsalted butter ~ in a saucepan. Crush the biscuits quite finely in a food processor or with a rolling pin. Place them in a bowl and stir in the hot melted butter. Press on to the base and sides of a 23cm/9in loose-based flan tin. Leave to set.

2 Make the filling. Place ~ the unopened can of condensed milk in a saucepan of boiling water and cover with a lid. Lower the heat and simmer for 2 hours, topping up the water as necessary. Do not allow to boil dry.

3 Remove the pan from ~ the heat and set aside, covered, until the can has cooled down completely in the water. Do not attempt to open the can until it is completely cold, as the contents will be under pressure due to the heat.

4 Melt the chocolate with ~ the crème fraîche or single cream and golden syrup in a heatproof bowl over simmering water. Stir in the caramelized condensed milk and beat until evenly mixed, then spread the filling over the base.

5 Slice the bananas and ~ arrange them over the chocolate filling.

6 Stir together the crème ~ fraîche and coffee, then spoon over the bananas. Decorate liberally with the chocolate curls.

GREEK CHOCOLATE MOUSSE TARTLETS

INGREDIENTS

1 quantity Chocolate Shortcrust Pastry

melted dark chocolate, to decorate

For the filling

200g/7oz white chocolate,
broken into squares

120ml/4fl oz/½ cup milk

10ml/2 tsp powdered gelatine

30ml/2 tbsp caster (superfine) sugar

5ml/1 tsp vanilla extract

2 eggs, separated

250g/9oz/generous 1 cup
Greek-style (US strained, plain) yogurt

~ SERVES 6 ~

Don't be fooled by the filling – it may be based on yogurt but it's just as sinful as all the other sweet sensations in this collection!

1 Preheat the oven to 190°C/375°F/Gas 5. Roll out the pastry and line six deep 10cm/4in loose-based flan tins.

2 Prick the base of each pastry case all over with a fork, cover with baking parchment, weigh down with baking beans, and bake blind for 10 minutes. Remove the beans and paper, return to the oven and bake for 10 minutes more, or until the pastry is firm. Leave to cool.

3 Make the filling. Melt the chocolate in a heatproof bowl over hot water. Pour the milk into a saucepan, sprinkle over the powdered gelatine and heat gently, stirring, until the gelatine has dissolved completely. Remove from the heat and stir in the chocolate.

COOK'S TIP
— • —

If you prefer, make a large tart instead of individual ones – use a 23cm/9in flan tin.

— • —

4 Whisk the sugar, vanilla extract and egg yolks in a large bowl, then beat in the chocolate mixture. Beat in the yogurt until evenly mixed. Chill until beginning to set.

5 Whisk the egg whites in a clean, grease-free bowl until stiff, then fold into the mixture. Divide among the pastry cases and leave to set.

6 Drizzle the melted chocolate over the tartlets to decorate.

CHOCOLATE PAVLOVA WITH PASSION FRUIT CREAM

INGREDIENTS

4 egg whites
200g/7oz/scant 1 cup caster (superfine) sugar
20ml/4 tsp cornflour (cornstarch)
45ml/3 tbsp cocoa powder
5ml/1 tsp vinegar
chocolate leaves, to decorate
For the filling
150g/5oz dark (semisweet) chocolate, broken into squares
250ml/8fl oz/1 cup double (heavy) cream
150g/5oz/⅔ cup Greek-style (US strained, plain) yogurt
2.5ml/½ tsp vanilla extract
4 passion fruit

☞ SERVES 6 ☜

Passion fruit is aptly named. Serve this superb sweet and anything could happen!

1 Preheat the oven to
~ 140°C/275°F/Gas 1.
Cut a piece of baking
parchment to fit a baking
sheet. Draw a 23cm/9in
circle on the paper and
place on the baking sheet.

2 Whisk the egg whites in
~ a clean bowl until stiff.
Gradually whisk in the sugar
and continue to whisk until
stiff. Whisk in the cornflour,
cocoa and vinegar.

3 Spread the mixture over
~ the marked circle,
making a slight dip in the
centre. Bake for 1½-2 hours.

4 Make the filling. Melt
~ the chocolate in a
heatproof bowl over hot
water, then remove from
the heat and cool slightly. In
a separate bowl, whip the
cream with the yogurt and
vanilla extract until thick.
Fold 60ml/4 tbsp into the
chocolate, then set both
mixtures aside.

5 Halve all the passion
~ fruit and scoop out the
pulp. Stir half into the plain
cream mixture. Carefully
remove the meringue shell
from the baking sheet and
place it on a large serving
plate. Fill with the passion
fruit cream, then spoon over
the chocolate mixture and
the remaining passion fruit.

6 Decorate with chocolate
~ leaves before serving.

> ### COOK'S TIP
>
> *The meringue can be
> baked a day in advance if
> necessary, and stored in
> an airtight container, but
> do not add the filling
> until about an hour
> before serving.*

MISSISSIPPI MUD PIE

Mud, mud, glorious mud – isn't that what the song says? Well, you can't get much more glorious than this!

1 Sift the flour into a bowl and rub in the butter until the mixture resembles coarse breadcrumbs. Stir in the egg yolks with just enough iced water to bind the mixture to a soft dough. Roll out on a lightly floured surface and line a deep 23cm/9in flan tin. Chill for about 30 minutes.

2 Preheat the oven to 190°C/375°F/Gas 5. Prick the pastry case all over with a fork, cover with greaseproof paper weighed down with baking beans and bake blind for 10 minutes. Remove the baking beans and paper, return to the oven and bake for a further 10 minutes, until the pastry is crisp and golden. Cool in the tin.

3 Make the filling. Mix the egg yolks, cornflour and 30ml/2 tbsp of the sugar in a bowl. Heat the milk in a saucepan until almost boiling, then beat into the egg mixture. Return to the clean pan and stir over a low heat until the custard has thickened and is smooth. Pour half the custard into a bowl.

4 Melt the chocolate in a heatproof bowl over hot water, then stir into the custard in the bowl, with the vanilla extract. Spread in the pastry case, cover closely to prevent the formation of a skin, cool, then chill until set.

5 Sprinkle the gelatine over the water in a small bowl, leave until spongy, then place over simmering water until all the gelatine has dissolved. Stir into the remaining custard, with the rum. Whisk the egg whites in a clean, grease-free bowl until stiff peaks form, whisk in the remaining sugar, then fold quickly into the custard before it sets.

6 Spoon the mixture over the chocolate custard to cover completely. Chill until set, then remove the pie from the tin and place on a serving plate. Spread whipped cream over the top and sprinkle with chocolate curls.

MANGO AND CHOCOLATE CREME BRULEE

INGREDIENTS

2 ripe mangoes

300ml/½ pint/1¼ cups double (heavy) cream

300ml/½ pint/1¼ cups crème fraîche

1 vanilla pod

115g/4oz dark (bittersweet) chocolate, broken into squares

4 egg yolks

15ml/1 tbsp clear honey

90ml/6 tbsp demerara (raw) sugar, for the topping

SERVES 6

Pure luxury — exotic fruit in a honeyed chocolate custard, topped with a crunchy coating of caramelized sugar.

1 Halve, stone (pit) and
~ peel the mangoes.
Roughly chop the flesh
and divide it among six
individual flameproof dishes
set on a baking sheet.

2 Mix the double cream
~ and crème fraîche in a
large heatproof bowl and
add the vanilla pod. Place
the bowl over a saucepan of
barely simmering water and
stir for about 10 minutes.
Do not let the bowl touch
the water or the cream may
overheat.

3 Remove the vanilla pod
~ from the bowl and stir in
the chocolate, a few pieces
at a time, until melted.
When the mixture is
completely smooth, remove
the bowl from the pan, but
leave the pan of water over
the heat.

4 Whisk the egg yolks and
~ clear honey in a second
heatproof bowl, then
gradually pour in the
chocolate cream, whisking
constantly. Place over the
pan of simmering water and
stir constantly until the
chocolate custard thickens
enough to coat the back of
a wooden spoon.

5 Remove from the heat
~ and spoon the custard
over the mangoes. Cool
completely, then chill in the
fridge until set.

6 Heat the grill (broiler) to
~ high. Sprinkle 15ml/
1 tbsp demerara sugar evenly
over each dessert and spray
lightly with a little water.

7 Grill (broil) briefly,
~ as close to the heat as
possible, until the sugar
melts and caramelizes.
Chill again before serving
the desserts.

COOK'S TIP

The mango and chocolate custard base can be prepared up to two days in advance. Make the caramelized sugar topping several hours before serving so that the desserts can be chilled.

CHOCOLATE HAZELNUT GALETTES

There's stacks of sophistication in these triple-tiered chocolate rounds sandwiched with a light creamy filling.

INGREDIENTS

175g/6oz dark (semisweet) chocolate, broken into squares

45ml/3 tbsp single (light) cream

30ml/2 tbsp flaked hazelnuts

115g/4oz white chocolate, broken into squares

175g/6oz/¾ cup crème fraîche

15ml/1 tbsp dry sherry

60ml/4 tbsp finely chopped hazelnuts, toasted

physalis (Cape gooseberries), dipped in white chocolate, to decorate

SERVES 4

1 Melt the dark chocolate in a heatproof bowl over hot water. Stir in the cream and remove from the heat.

2 Draw 12 x 7.5cm/3in circles on sheets of baking parchment. Turn the paper over and spread the dark chocolate over each marked circle, covering in a thin, even layer. Scatter flaked hazelnuts over the circles, then leave until set.

3 Melt the white chocolate in a heatproof bowl over hot water, then stir in the crème fraîche and dry sherry. Fold in the chopped, toasted hazelnuts. Leave to cool, then chill in the refrigerator until the mixture holds its shape.

4 Remove the dark chocolate rounds from the paper and sandwich together in stacks of three, spooning the white chocolate hazelnut cream between each layer and using the hazelnut-covered rounds on top. Chill.

5 To serve, place the galettes on individual plates and decorate with chocolate-dipped physalis.

COOK'S TIP

Make heart shapes for a special Valentine's Day dessert.

$\mathcal{S}$WEETS AND DRINKS

Chocolate truffles, nutty fudge and liqueur-spiked moulded chocs and candies are simple and rewarding to make, and, packed into pretty boxes or jars, they make wonderful gifts. For after-dinner sweet treats, Cognac and Ginger Creams or Peppermint Chocolate Sticks are so much more special than bought mints. If you prefer liquid chocolate, at the end of the day you can sink into a comfy armchair with a warming glass of Irish Chocolate Velvet or Mexican Hot Chocolate.

CHOCOLATE AND CHERRY COLETTES

INGREDIENTS

115g/4oz dark (bittersweet) chocolate, broken into squares

75g/3oz white or milk chocolate, broken into squares

25g/1oz/2 tbsp unsalted butter, melted

15ml/1 tbsp Kirsch or brandy

60ml/4 tbsp double (heavy) cream

18-20 maraschino cherries or liqueur-soaked cherries

milk chocolate curls, to decorate

MAKES 18–20

For a sweet surprise for a friend or lover, pack these pretty little sweets in a decorative box.

3 Place one cherry in each chocolate case. Spoon the white or milk chocolate cream mixture into a piping bag fitted with a small star nozzle and pipe over the cherries mounded in a generous swirl.

4 Top each colette with a chocolate curl. Leave until set, then chill in the fridge until needed.

COOK'S TIP

If foil sweet (candy) cases are difficult to find, use double thickness mini paper sweet (candy) cases instead.

1 Melt the dark chocolate in a bowl over hot water, then remove from the heat. Spoon into 18-20 foil sweet (candy) cases, spread evenly up the sides with a small brush, then leave in a cool place to set.

2 Melt the white or milk chocolate with the butter in a heatproof bowl over hot water. Remove from the heat and stir in the Kirsch or brandy, then the cream. Cool until the mixture is thick enough to hold its shape.

COGNAC AND GINGER CREAMS

INGREDIENTS

300g/11oz dark (bittersweet) chocolate, broken into squares

45ml/3 tbsp double (heavy) cream

30ml/2 tbsp cognac

15ml/1 tbsp stem ginger syrup

4 pieces stem ginger, finely chopped

crystallized ginger, to decorate

MAKES 18–20

Only you know the secret of these handsome hand-made chocolates: that the mysterious dark exterior conceals a glorious ginger and cognac cream filling.

1 Polish the insides of about 18-20 chocolate moulds with cotton wool. Melt about two-thirds of the chocolate in a heatproof bowl over hot water, then spoon a little into each mould. Reserve a little of the melted chocolate, for sealing the creams.

2 Using a small brush, sweep the chocolate up the sides of the moulds to coat them evenly, then invert them on to a sheet of baking parchment and leave to set.

3 Melt the remaining chocolate, and mix in the cream, cognac, ginger syrup and stem ginger. Spoon into the chocolate-lined moulds. Warm the reserved chocolate if necessary, then spoon a little into each mould to seal. Leave in a cool place (not the fridge) until set.

4 To remove the chocolates from the moulds, gently press them out on to a cool surface. Decorate with small pieces of crystallized ginger.

COOK'S TIP

Simple chocolate moulds can be bought in most good kitchen shops and give a highly professional finish. Polishing the moulds thoroughly with fine cotton wool results in really glossy chocolates that are relatively easy to turn out. If they do stick, put them in the fridge for a short time, then try again. Don't chill them for too long, or you may dull the surface of the chocolate.

CHOCOLATE FONDANT HEARTS

Get set to impress with these luscious love tokens. If you want to be really corny, pipe both sets of initials on each one.

INGREDIENTS

60ml/4 tbsp liquid glucose

50g/2oz dark (bittersweet) chocolate, broken into squares

50g/2oz white chocolate, broken into squares

1 egg white, lightly beaten

450g/1lb/3½ cups icing (confectioners') sugar, sifted

melted dark (bittersweet) and white chocolate, to decorate

MAKES ABOUT 50

1 Divide the glucose ~ between two heatproof bowls. Place each bowl over hot water and heat gently, then add the dark chocolate to one bowl and the white chocolate to the other. Leave until the chocolate has completely melted.

2 Remove both bowls ~ from the heat and cool slightly. Add half the egg white to each bowl, then divide the icing sugar between them, mixing to combine well.

3 Knead each mixture ~ separately with your hands until it is smooth and pliable. On a surface lightly dusted with icing sugar, roll out both mixtures separately to a thickness of about 3mm/⅛in.

4 Brush the surface of the ~ dark chocolate fondant with egg white and place the white chocolate fondant on top. Roll the surface lightly with a rolling pin to press the pieces together.

5 Using a small heart- ~ shaped cutter, stamp out about 50 hearts from the fondant. Drizzle melted chocolate over each heart to decorate and leave until cool and firm.

COOK'S TIP

Don't throw away the fondant trimmings – knead them together to create a marbled effect, roll the fondant out again and cut out more hearts or other shapes to use as cake decorations.

$\mathcal{M}$ ALT WHISKY TRUFFLES

These tempting truffles make perfect presents – if you can part with them.

INGREDIENTS

200g/7oz dark (bittersweet) chocolate, broken into squares

150ml/¼ pint/⅔ cup double (heavy) cream

45ml/3 tbsp malt whisky

115g/4oz/1 cup icing (confectioners') sugar

cocoa powder, for coating

MAKES 25–30

3 Stir in the chocolate and
~ icing sugar, mixing
evenly, then leave until firm
enough to handle.

1 Melt the chocolate in a
~ heatproof bowl over hot
water, then cool slightly.

4 Dust your hands with
~ cocoa and shape the
mixture into bite-size balls.
Coat in cocoa powder and
pack into pretty cases or
boxes. Store in the fridge
for up to 3–4 days if
necessary.

2 Whip the cream with
~ the whisky in a bowl
until thick enough to hold
its shape.

145

CHOCOLATE ALMOND TORRONNE

Serve this speciality in thin slices.

INGREDIENTS

115g/4oz dark (semisweet) chocolate, broken into squares

50g/2oz/4 tbsp unsalted butter

1 egg white

115g/4oz/½ cup caster (superfine) sugar

50g/2oz/½ cup ground almonds

75g/3oz/½ cup chopped toasted almonds

75ml/5 tbsp chopped candied peel

For the coating

175g/6oz white chocolate, broken into squares

25g/1oz/2 tbsp unsalted butter

115g/4oz/1 cup flaked almonds, toasted

MAKES ABOUT 20 SLICES

COOK'S TIP

The mixture can be shaped into a simple round roll instead of the triangular shape if you prefer.

1 Melt the chocolate with ~ the butter in a heatproof bowl over barely simmering water until smooth.

2 In a clean, grease-free ~ bowl, whisk the egg white with the sugar until stiff. Gradually beat in the melted chocolate, then stir in the ground almonds, chopped almonds and peel.

3 Tip the mixture on to a ~ large sheet of non-stick baking paper and shape into a thick roll.

4 As the mixture cools, ~ use the paper to press the roll firmly into a triangular shape. Twist the paper over the triangular roll and chill until completely set.

5 Make the coating. Melt ~ the white chocolate with the butter in a heatproof bowl over hot water. Unwrap the chocolate roll and spread the white chocolate quickly over the surface. Press the almonds in a thin even coating over the chocolate, working quickly before the chocolate sets.

6 Chill again until firm, ~ then cut the torronne into thin slices to serve.

R ICH CHOCOLATE PISTACHIO FUDGE

Make a big batch of this meltingly rich chocolate fudge packed with pistachios – it won't last long!

INGREDIENTS

250g/9oz/generous 1 cup white sugar

375g/13oz can sweetened condensed milk

50g/2oz/4 tbsp unsalted butter

5ml/1 tsp vanilla extract

115g/4oz dark (semisweet) chocolate, grated

75g/3oz/¾ cup pistachios

MAKES 36

1 Grease a 19cm/7½in
~ square cake tin and line
with baking parchment.
Mix the sugar, condensed
milk and butter in a heavy-
based pan. Heat gently,
stirring, until the sugar has
dissolved completely.

2 Bring the mixture to the
~ boil, stirring occasionally,
and boil until it registers
116°C/240°F on a sugar
thermometer.

3 Remove the pan from
~ the heat and beat in the
vanilla extract, chocolate
and nuts. Beat vigorously
until smooth and creamy.

4 Pour the mixture into
~ the prepared cake tin
and spread evenly. Leave
until just set, then mark
into squares. Leave to set
completely before cutting
into squares and removing
from the tin. Store the
fudge in an airtight
container in a cool place.

COOK'S TIP

*If you haven't got a
sugar thermometer, test
the mixture by dropping
a small spoonful into a
cup of iced water. If you
can roll the mixture to a
soft ball with your
fingertips, the fudge
is ready.*

CHOCOLATE-COATED NUT BRITTLE

INGREDIENTS

115g/4oz/1 cup mixed pecan nuts
and whole almonds

115g/4oz/½ cup caster (superfine)
sugar

60ml/4 tbsp water

200g/7 oz dark (bittersweet) chocolate,
broken into squares

MAKES 24 PIECES

Take equal amounts of pecan nuts and almonds, set them in crisp caramel, then add a dark chocolate coating for a sweet that's sensational.

1 Lightly grease a baking
~ sheet with butter or oil.
Mix the nuts, sugar and
water in a heavy-based
saucepan. Place the pan over
a gentle heat, stirring
without boiling until the
sugar has dissolved.

2 Bring to the boil, then
~ lower the heat to
moderate and cook until the
mixture turns a rich golden
brown and registers
148°C/300°F on a sugar or
candy thermometer. To test
without a thermometer,
drop a few drops of the
mixture into a cup of iced
water. The mixture should
become brittle enough to
snap with your fingers.

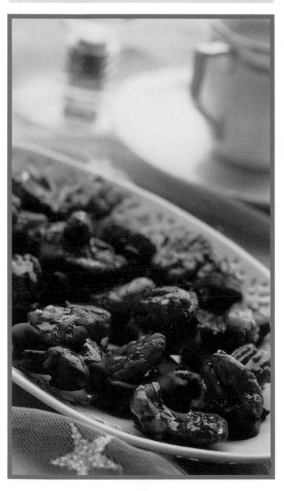

3 Quickly remove the pan
~ from the heat and tip the
mixture on to the prepared
baking sheet, spreading it
evenly. Leave until
completely cold and hard.

4 Break the nut brittle
~ into bite-size pieces.
Melt the chocolate in a
heatproof bowl over hot
water and dip the pieces to
half-coat them. Leave on a
sheet of non-stick baking
paper to set.

COOK'S TIP

*These look best in rough
chunks, so don't worry if
the pieces break unevenly,
or if there are gaps in the
chocolate coating.*

PEPPERMINT CHOCOLATE STICKS

Turn the lights down low, curl up on the couch and pamper yourself with these delicious bite-size chocolate sticks.

INGREDIENTS

115g/4oz/½ cup white sugar

150ml/¼ pint/⅔ cup water

2.5ml/½ tsp peppermint extract

200g/7oz dark (bittersweet) chocolate, broken into squares

60ml/4 tbsp toasted desiccated (unsweetened shredded) coconut

MAKES ABOUT 80

1 Lightly oil a large baking sheet. Place the sugar and water in a small, heavy-based saucepan and heat gently, stirring occasionally, until the sugar has dissolved.

2 Bring to the boil and boil rapidly without stirring until the syrup registers 137°C/280°F on a sugar or candy thermometer. Remove the pan from the heat and add the peppermint extract, then pour on to the greased baking sheet and leave until set and cold.

3 Break the peppermint mixture into a small bowl and use the end of a rolling pin to crush it into small pieces.

4 Melt the chocolate in a heatproof bowl over hot water. Remove from the heat and stir in the mint pieces and desiccated coconut.

5 Lay a 30 x 25cm/12 x 10in sheet of baking parchment on a flat surface. Spread the chocolate mixture over the paper, leaving a narrow border all around, to make a rectangle measuring about 25 x 20cm/ 10 x 8in. Leave to set. When firm, use a sharp knife to cut into thin sticks, each about 6cm/2½in long.

COOK'S TIP

The set chocolate mixture could be cut into squares instead, to eat just as they are, or for decorating cakes and desserts.

MEXICAN HOT CHOCOLATE

Snuggle down in bed with a big mug of spicy hot chocolate. In Mexico, this drink is traditionally whisked with a carved wooden beater called a molinillo, but a modern blender works just as well.

INGREDIENTS

1 litre/1¾ pints/4 cups milk

1 cinnamon stick

2 whole cloves

115g/4oz dark (semisweet) chocolate, broken into squares

2-3 drops of almond extract

~ SERVES 4 ~

1 Heat the milk gently ~ with the spices in a saucepan until almost boiling, then stir in the dark chocolate over a moderate heat until melted.

2 Strain into a blender, ~ add the almond extract and whizz on high speed for about 30 seconds until frothy. Alternatively, whisk the mixture with a hand-held electric mixer.

3 Pour into warmed ~ heatproof glasses and serve immediately.

COOK'S TIP

If you don't have whole cinnamon and cloves, add a pinch of each of the ground spices to the mixture before whisking.

IRISH CHOCOLATE VELVET

> *Warm the cockles of your heart with this smooth, sophisticated drink.*

INGREDIENTS

120ml/4fl oz/½ cup double (heavy) cream

400ml/14fl oz/1¾ cups milk

115g/4 oz milk chocolate, broken into squares

30ml/2 tbsp cocoa powder

60ml/4 tbsp Irish whiskey

whipped cream, for topping

chocolate curls, to decorate

~ SERVES 4 ~

1 ~ Whip the cream in a bowl until it is thick enough to hold its shape.

2 ~ Place the milk and chocolate in a saucepan and heat gently, stirring, until the chocolate has completely melted.

3 ~ Whisk in the cocoa, then bring to the boil, remove from the heat and add the whipped cream and Irish whiskey.

4 ~ Pour quickly into four warmed mugs or heatproof glasses and top each serving with a generous spoonful of whipped cream. Decorate with chocolate curls.

COOK'S TIP

If Irish whiskey is not available, use Scotch whisky, brandy or a liqueur based on either.

ICED MINT AND CHOCOLATE COOLER

Many chocolate drinks are warm and comforting, but this one is really refreshing – ideal for a hot summer's day.

INGREDIENTS

60ml/4 tbsp drinking chocolate (hot cocoa mix)

400ml/14fl oz/1¾ cups chilled milk

150ml/5fl oz/⅔ cup natural (plain) yogurt

2.5ml/½ tsp peppermint extract

4 scoops chocolate ice cream

mint leaves and chocolate shapes, to decorate

SERVES 4

2 Pour into a cold bowl or large jug and whisk in the remaining milk, yogurt and peppermint extract.

1 Place the drinking chocolate in a pan and stir in about 120ml/4fl oz/ ½ cup of the milk. Heat stirring, until near boiling, then remove from the heat.

3 Pour the mixture into four tall glasses and top each with a scoop of ice cream. Decorate with mint leaves and chocolate shapes. Serve immediately.

COOK'S TIP

Use cocoa powder instead of drinking chocolate, but add sugar to taste.

*B*ASIC RECIPES

Chocolate Ganache

A luxurious, creamy frosting for cakes, gâteaux and desserts.

ENOUGH TO COVER A 23CM/9IN ROUND CAKE
250ml/8fl oz/1 cup double (heavy) cream
225g/8oz dark (semisweet) chocolate, broken into squares

1 Heat the cream and
~ chocolate together in a saucepan over a low heat, stirring frequently until the chocolate has melted. Pour into a bowl, leave to cool, then whisk until the mixture begins to hold its shape.

Chocolate Buttercream

A quick, everyday filling and frosting.

ENOUGH TO FILL A 20CM/8IN ROUND CAKE
75g/3oz/6 tbsp unsalted butter, softened
175g/6 oz/1½ cups icing (confectioners') sugar
15ml/1 tbsp cocoa powder
2.5ml/½ tsp vanilla extract

1 Place all the ingredients
~ in a large bowl.

2 Beat well to a smooth,
~ spreadable consistency.

White Chocolate Frosting

A fluffy, rich, white frosting for cakes and gâteaux.

ENOUGH TO COVER A 20CM/8IN ROUND CAKE
175g/6oz white chocolate, broken into squares
75g/3oz/6 tbsp unsalted butter
115g/4oz/1 cup icing (confectioners') sugar
90ml/6 tbsp double (heavy) cream

1 Melt the chocolate with
~ the butter in a heatproof bowl over hot water. Remove from the heat and beat in the icing sugar.

2 Whip the cream in a
~ separate bowl until it just holds its shape, then beat into the chocolate mixture. Allow the mixture to cool, stirring occasionally, until it begins to hold its shape. Use immediately.

*V*ARIATION

For a special occasion cake, stir in a tablespoon of brandy or your favourite liqueur.

Chocolate Fondant

Easily moulded, this icing gives a smooth finish to celebration cakes, and can also be made into flowers, shapes or cut-outs for decoration.

ENOUGH TO COVER AND DECORATE
A 23CM/9IN ROUND CAKE
350g/12oz dark (bittersweet) chocolate, broken into squares
60ml/4 tbsp liquid glucose
2 egg whites
900g/2lb/7 cups icing (confectioners') sugar

1 Melt the chocolate
~ with the glucose in a heatproof bowl over hot water. Stir to mix, remove from the heat and cool.

2 In a clean, grease-free
~ bowl, whisk the egg whites, then stir into the chocolate with 45ml/3 tbsp of the icing sugar.

3 Using an electric mixer,
~ gradually beat in enough of the remaining icing sugar to make a stiff paste. Wrap in clear film if not using immediately.

Glossy Chocolate Sauce

Delicious poured over ice cream or on hot or cold desserts.

SERVES 6
115g/4oz/½ cup caster (superfine) sugar
60ml/4 tbsp water
175g/6oz dark (bittersweet) chocolate, broken into squares
30ml/2 tbsp unsalted butter
30ml/2 tbsp brandy or orange juice

1 Place the sugar and
~ water in a saucepan and heat gently, stirring occasionally, until the sugar has dissolved.

2 Stir in the chocolate, a
~ few squares at a time, until melted, then add the butter in the same way. Do not allow the sauce to boil. Stir in the brandy or orange juice and serve warm.

COOK'S TIP

This sauce freezes well. Pour into a freezer-proof container, seal, label and freeze for up to 3 months. Thaw at room temperature.

White Chocolate Sauce

Rich and sweet, this makes a lovely contrast to a dark, bitter chocolate mousse or pudding.

SERVES 6

150ml/¼ pint/⅔ cup double (heavy) cream
150g/5oz white chocolate, broken into squares
30ml/2 tbsp brandy or Cointreau

1
~ Heat the cream in a saucepan over a low heat until almost boiling.

2
~ Stir in the chocolate, a few squares at a time, until melted and smooth. Remove from the heat and stir in the brandy or Cointreau before serving.

Variations

WHITE MOCHA SAUCE: *Stir in 30ml/2 tbsp strong black coffee just before serving.*
COCONUT CHOCOLATE CREAM SAUCE: *Stir in 45ml/3 tbsp powdered or liquid coconut cream just before serving.*

Chocolate Shortcrust Pastry (1)

A rich, dark, chocolate-flavoured pastry for sweet flans and tarts.

115g/4oz dark (bittersweet) chocolate, broken into squares
225g/8oz/2 cups plain (all-purpose) flour
115g/4oz/½ cup unsalted butter
15-30ml/1-2 tbsp cold water

1 Melt the chocolate in a heatproof bowl over hot water.
~ Allow to cool but not set.

2 Place the flour in a
~ mixing bowl. Rub in the butter until the mixture resembles fine breadcrumbs.

3 Make a well in the
~ centre of the mixture. Add the cooled chocolate, with just enough cold water to mix to a firm dough.

Chocolate Shortcrust Pastry (2)

An alternative sweet chocolate pastry, this time made with the addition of cocoa instead of chocolate.

175g/6oz/1½ cups plain (all-purpose) flour
30ml/2 tbsp cocoa powder
30ml/2 tbsp icing (confectioners') sugar
115g/4oz/½ cup butter
15-30ml/1-2 tbsp cold water

1 Sift the flour, cocoa and icing sugar into a bowl.
~

2 Place the butter in a pan with the water and heat gently
~ until just melted. Cool.

3 Stir into the flour to make a smooth dough. Chill until
~ firm, then roll out and use as required.

Chocolate Baskets or Cups

These impressive baskets make pretty, edible containers for mousse or ice cream.

MAKES 6
175g/6oz dark (bittersweet), milk, or white chocolate
25g/1oz/2 tbsp butter

1 Cut out six 15cm/6in rounds from baking parchment.

2 Melt the chocolate with the butter in a heatproof bowl over barely simmering water. Stir until smooth. Spoon one-sixth of the chocolate over each round, spreading it to an 2cm/¾in of the edge.

3 Carefully lift each covered paper round and drape it over an upturned cup or ramekin, curving the edges to create a frilled effect.

4 Leave until completely set, then carefully lift off the chocolate shape and peel away the paper.

5 For a different effect, brush the chocolate over, leaving the edges jagged.

Chocolate-dipped Fruit

Strawberries, grapes, cherries and other small fruits taste absolutely delicious when fully or partially coated in chocolate, as do mandarin segments. Fruit for dipping should be ripe but not soft, and clean and dry. Whole nuts such as almonds or brazils can also be dipped.

1 Melt the chocolate and remove from the heat. Dip the fruits or nuts fully or halfway into the chocolate and allow the excess to drip off.

2 Place on a baking sheet lined with non-stick baking paper and leave until completely set.

Chocolate Squiggles

Melt a quantity of chocolate and spread fairly thinly over a cool, smooth surface. Leave until just set, then draw a citrus zester firmly across the surface to remove curls or "squiggles" of the chocolate.

ℐNDEX